DEVELOPING PARENT & COMMUNITY UNDERSTANDING OF PERFORMANCE-BASED ASSESSMENT

Kathryn Anderson Alvestad

EYE ON EDUCATION

6 DEPOT WAY WEST, SUITE 106

LARCHMONT, NY 10538

(914) 833–0551

(914) 833–0761 fax

www.eyeoneducation.com

Library of Congress Cataloging-in-Publication Data

Alvestad, Kathryn Anderson, 1948–
     Developing parent and community understanding of performance-based assessment / Kathryn Anderson Alvestad.
          p. cm.
     ISBN 1-930556-02-0
     1. Competency based educational tests—United States. 2. Home and school—United States. 3. Community and school—United States. I. Title

LC1034.A48 2000
370.19—dc21

00-28777

10 9 8 7 6 5 4 3 2 1

Editorial and production services provided by
Richard H. Adin Freelance Editorial Services
52 Oakwood Blvd., Poughkeepsie, NY 12603-4112
(914-471-3566)

MEET THE AUTHOR

Kathryn Anderson Alvestad, principal of Dowell Elementary School in Calvert County, Maryland, served as supervisor and then as director of accountability and testing for Calvert County for seven years. She has consulted on performance assessment for numerous schools and school districts. She is the author of several articles on technology and assessment topics. Prior to her work in the field of assessment, she taught in the primary grades for six years and served as an elementary school vice principal for eight years. She has also taught at the undergraduate and graduate levels for the University of Maryland, Western Maryland College, and the College of Notre Dame of Maryland.

FOREWORD

In this book, Kathryn Alvestad offers us the benefit of her years of experience in helping parents understand the rationale for using performance-based assessments. She provides specific and practical advice, illustrated by clear examples and enhanced by humor and common sense.

This unique book provides proven strategies to help parents see where performance assessment fits in the big picture of standards-based education and student learning. The suggestions in this book can be applied in a variety of settings, including one-to-one conferences with parents, PTSA meetings, and school board sessions. They can easily be adjusted to fit the particular needs of parents or educators. Most importantly, they work.

If you seek to help parents better understand the goals and benefits of performance-based assessment, you'll find this book to be a valuable resource.

Jay McTighe

TABLE OF CONTENTS

PREFACE

Due to an overhaul of the educational accountability program that resulted in two new assessment programs, educators in Maryland have been doing a lot of re-educating in the last 10 years. It became obvious early on that the task of helping parents and the community understand and accept the new assessments was going to be more complicated than anyone ever expected.

The process for helping parents and other community members understand performance-based assessment that is outlined here, got its start in Calvert County, Maryland, as a response to the mandated state-level changes. It has been shared with educators across the U.S. at numerous conferences and professional meetings. Continuously revised over a period of five years, it has had the advantage of input from educators all over the country and has been enriched continuously as a result.

One of the first things we learned when we initiated the process was that past practice would not work in this situation. We could not simply make a presentation at a PTA meeting or plan a workshop and expect that parents and members of our community would walk away with the information and skills they needed in order to become full partners in the new initiative. In the first place, we had to get past a lot of anxiety and frustration that resulted from the speed with which the state implemented the program. In addition, we were dealing with understandings and skills that were new to *us*, let alone to our parents and community! So we found ourselves starting *at scratch* and moving forward carefully, as our audience became ready for each new step.

Because of the unique nature of the roadblocks to success for performance-based assessment, education professionals need clear and proven guidance on how to overcome the roadblocks and replace them with support and involvement on the part of parents in particular and the community in general. This book provides that guidance. It is intended for education professionals, primarily principals, but also for others who work at the building and central office levels.

The format of the book is intended to take the reader step-by-step through the process of helping adults understand performance-based assessment. It outlines the basic information parents and the community need in order to support the school/school system both fundamentally (in thought) and practically (in action). The goal is to take parents (and the community) from *uninformed* to *informed and actively involved*.

Chapter 1 sets the stage by explaining why changing times are leading to changes in practice. The text could actually be used as an introductory speech at a staff meeting. Chapter 2 describes the basic principles of effective strategies for helping parents and the community understand the methodology. It covers the importance of leadership, the importance of a consistent approach in the school and the home, and describes various roles which you can expect parents to be able to play as teachers of their children. It includes a detailed description of information needed by parents and the community in order to have a basic understanding of performance-based assessment. Some general principles of delivery are presented, and a brief discussion of potential roadblocks to success concludes the chapter.

Chapters 3, 4, 5, and 6 provide detailed descriptions of the four steps in the process for developing parent and community understanding of performance-based assessment. Each chapter describes recommendations for what to do, how to do it, and when to do it. Examples of successful implementation strategies from school systems in Maryland as well as from other school systems with which we have shared the process are also included.

Chapter 7 presents some ideas for maintaining communication with parents and the community after the initial phase of the process has been completed.

Many individuals provided support and inspiration to the author throughout this project. I am deeply indebted to Teacher Specialists Lynne Pachico and Valerie Weems-Garber for their technical assistance and personal support. Sincere thanks are due to Dr. Judith Dorsch Backes, Dr. Carolyn Wood, Dr. Mary Kay Armour, and Jay McTighe for their continuous professional support and assistance as the project unfolded. The project could not have been accomplished without the support of many administrators and teachers in the Calvert County, Maryland Public Schools, including Dr. James R. Hook, superintendent, and Dr. J. Kenneth Horsmon, deputy superintendent. Last, but not least, my husband and daughters have been my inspiration from the very beginning and have supported me every step of the way.

1

INTRODUCING PERFORMANCE-BASED ASSESSMENT: CHANGING TIMES REQUIRE CHANGES IN PRACTICE

Much of the criticism directed at schools over the past few years has revolved around their supposed inability to produce workers with the kinds of employability skills that are needed for an information-rich, dynamic workplace. High School graduates purportedly cannot read, write, communicate, cooperate, and independently solve problems well enough to be efficient workers. Most of all, they are apparently not lifelong learners capable of adapting to the constant changes that the Information Age engenders. Reports imply that employers resent having to spend time and money *retrofitting* new employees with the skills needed.

Proponents of performance-based assessment believe that a shift to this form of assessing will have major impact on the skill development of students and therefore alleviate some of the problems most insidious in our workforce.

Major shifts in instructional practice require a rethinking of every aspect of what we do, from the approach we take to school readiness to the requirements for graduation. We especially have to re-evaluate our use of resources, both financial and human. In the face of declining resources, educators have been forced to try to seek out and make efficient use of other sources of support. Financial resources often come in the form of grants and other bequests from sources outside the community. Human resources, however, usually come from the community itself—those individuals who are most invested in the success of the schools attended by their children, grandchildren, neighbors, and potential employees.

1

Parents and other adults in the community are a rich resource that is often overlooked as schools adjust to major changes, and this is unfortunate because their involvement can be a critical piece in the puzzle.

> **Parents are a rich resource that is often overlooked in the school improvement formula.**

WHY IS PARENT INVOLVEMENT IMPORTANT?

Studies on school and family connections have shown over and over again that parent involvement "…raises the academic achievement of students, improves attitudes and performance of children in school, helps parents understand the work of the school, enables parents and children to communicate more and show their caring toward each other, and builds school-community relationships in an ongoing, problem-preventing way" (Rich & Jones, 1985, pp. 9–10). Supportive home environments help children succeed in school in two ways: "(1) Children work successfully toward goals and values when they recognize that the attitudes and expectations of both home and school overlap, and (2) children's academic achievement improves when families demonstrate their connection to school goals by encouraging their children's intellectual development, studying with them, showing approval of school activities, and respecting their children's efforts" (Fruchter, Galletta, & White, 1993, p. 36). Under ordinary circumstances, these benefits serve to enhance the education of students, but in situations where significant changes are occurring in the fundamental way in which education is accomplished, they can make the difference between success and failure.

WHAT HAPPENS WHEN MAJOR SHIFTS IN PRACTICE OCCUR?

One of the first things some educators anticipate when new methods of assessment are implemented is that student achievement will decline, at least until everyone becomes accustomed to the new methodology.

The next thing we are likely to anticipate is that students' attitudes will suffer because of the confusion that the new methodology fosters. We know that young children, especially, may be disturbed by changes in methodology they have come to think of as routine.

Most likely we also assume that parents and community members will not understand the new methodology and therefore call our methods and motivation into question. Sometimes we actually gear up for the criticism so that we can meet it head on and be ready with our defense mechanisms when the inevitable avalanche of negative outcry ensues.

When new methods of assessment are implemented we sometimes fail to envision the controversies that will occur at home as our students try to explain to their parents that, "The teacher says I'm supposed to do it *this* way!" Though a certain amount of this type of controversy occurs inevitably, the more comprehensive the change, the worse it can be. Unfortunately, it is frequently the last thing we consider when making plans for change.

HOW CAN WE AVOID PROBLEMS?

The best way to ensure that *all of the above* will *not* occur is to begin any new initiative with a clear plan for parent and community education and involvement. Doing so can help assure that student achievement will remain high or even improve, student attitude and performance will remain at it's maximum, parents and community members will understand and support the new initiative, parents and students will continue to communicate effectively, and school-community relations will be strengthened.

> The best way to ensure that predictable problems will *not* occur is to begin any new initiative with a clear plan for parent and community education and involvement.

WHAT ARE THE KEYS TO EFFECTIVE PARENT INVOLVEMENT?

Parent involvement is most effective when it is comprehensive, long lasting, and well planned. (Henderson, Marburger, & Ooms, 1987, p.10) A proactive approach is essential to the success of any new initiative, and this is especially so in the case of performance-based assessment. We need to enter the implementation process with a clear understanding of the needs of our parent and community population so that our approach can be comprehensive. We need to budget the time needed to implement the parent/community component of our efforts so that the effects will be long lasting. And we need to involve all stakeholders in the planning so that the results will meet everyone's needs adequately and effectively.

A Proactive Approach

♦ **A clear understanding of the needs of the population.**

♦ **Budgeted time needed for implementation.**

♦ **Involvement of all stakeholders.**

Yet the solution is not that simple. The increased use of performance-based assessment in today's schools has presented unique problems in terms of parent and community involvement. Not only are schools and school systems faced with the skepticism and resistance that usually accompanies *any* new initiative, they are also faced with overcoming the fear and anxiety with which most adults face the concept of tests. Assessment, in general, frightens almost all adults for one reason or another. We dislike being assessed, and sometimes become anxious merely at the mention of the word *test*. Worse yet, many adults think performance-based assessment is something new. The fear, anxiety, and lack of understanding surrounding performance-based assessment keep some adults from accepting it as a realistic, valid, and meaningful method for determining what students have learned and are able to do.

Yet we know, as Joyce Epstein has said, "All the years that children attend school, they also attend home" (1990, p. 99). Academic achievement is higher and attitudes about school are more positive when parents are aware, knowledgeable, and encouraging about school. Unfortunately, it is difficult to be aware, knowledgeable, and encouraging when you are also fearful, anxious, and unsure.

Parents are their children's first teachers. They teach their children from the time they are babies and continue to teach them what they think is important for as long as the children remain in their care. (McGilp & Michael, 1994, p. 5) How do they know how to do this? They rely on what they experienced themselves as children and as students, and they do what comes naturally. Most human beings are born with a certain amount of curiosity, and it is a natural thing to try to find out about something by taking it apart, experiencing it with the senses, experimenting with it, and trying to put it back together. Parents help their children learn simply by being learners themselves and guiding their children through the experience of exploring new things. They also teach their children by example, modeling behaviors and habits that their children observe day in and day out. True, sometimes what parents teach their children is negative in nature, such as unhealthy habits and bad attitudes. But the fact remains that parents are their children's first and most influential teachers. "Parents provide the continuity that children need to succeed as they progress through the education system, and help to integrate children's experience at home, at school, and in the community" (Fruchter et al., 1993, p. 36). Even if they are not able to help directly with schoolwork like advanced mathematics and the correct format for bibliography entries, they create an environment at home that either supports or does not support the school, they model positive attitudes toward education, and they share educational activities with their children. (Jones, 1991, p. 11) They teach by encouragement, demonstration, modeling, revising and monitoring children's efforts. When they know their children have acquired a skill, they encourage them to use it freely and independently. "Parents know how to build on what children know, show them other ways, correct and praise children's efforts, and give them further opportunities for practice" (McGilp & Michael, 1994, p. 6). These things are all essential elements of a good education and the lack of them can make the difference between success and failure for many students.

If parents do not understand innovations, do not have the information needed to model positive attitudes, and do not have the skills needed to share educational activities with their children, they cannot provide the support needed by the school when new initiatives are under way.

THE CHALLENGE AHEAD

Rioux and Berla have stated that "...parent-family involvement is a dimension of enormous potential that has too long been ignored and has not received the attention and respect it deserves" (1993, p. 3). They believe that we are at a point in time when parent-family involvement could expand dramatically and contribute significantly to our school improvement efforts. This is opportune because the changes brought about by our use of more performance-based techniques have the potential to revolutionize how much and how well students learn. An expansion of parent and community involvement could significantly enhance the success of this initiative as well as set a new standard for future initiatives.

"Involving parents early—and continuing that involvement throughout the school-age years—in the education of their children at home and at school is one of the most challenging tasks educators face; but it holds the greatest potential for significantly increasing children's social, affective, and academic growth and achievement" (Jones, 1991, p. 7). When the way in which we educate changes significantly, the challenge is even greater. When the way in which we educate changes so drastically that even we who do the *lion's share* of the teaching have to readjust our thinking and way of doing things, the challenge becomes enormous. We not only have to think about and prepare for the re-education of our staff, but at the same time, we have to think about and prepare for the re-education of our parents and community. It is in this aspect of preparing for and implementing change that we in education often err. We direct our attention to the staff first and assume we can address the needs of the parents and community later. When educational initiatives fail, part of the reason is that planning and implementation for staff and community are not approached as an integrated process. In the current era of change, it is imperative that schools and school systems think about and prepare for the needs of parents and the community at the same time as they are thinking about and preparing for changes in assessment strategies and the expectations for instructional practice. In the words of Rioux and Berla, it is "crucial that parents be involved from the beginning in understanding and accepting the new vision, so that they will enthusiastically choose to have their children participate..." (1993, p. 258).

2

SOME BASIC PRINCIPLES

If you are a leader in a school system or state that has embraced the methodology of performance-based assessment system-wide, the basic concepts you will need to get started involving parents may have been defined in advance and described in literature provided by the decision-making source. If not, the contents of this chapter will serve as a good *jumping off point* for your efforts to get parents and the community involved.

THE IMPORTANCE OF LEADERSHIP

The role of the school administrator in the success or failure of any new initiative cannot be taken for granted. The acceptance, smooth implementation, and overall success of new initiatives are contingent upon the leadership of a *knowledgeable, enthusiastic,* and *persistent* leader. Indeed, "…if the leadership is cautious, has low energy, and is ambivalent about potential outcomes," programs are unlikely to be successful (Rioux & Berla, 1993, p. 330).

KNOWLEDGE

It is important for school leaders to be as familiar with the principles and practices of performance-based assessment as possible. Although the literature on the subject was scarce until a few years ago, there are now numerous books on the topic. Figure 2.1 is a list of several that are particularly recommended because of their clarity.

FIGURE 2.1 RECOMMENDED BOOKS ON ASSESSMENT

Burke, K. (1993). *The mindful school: How to assess authentic learning.* Palatine, IL: IRI Skylight Publishing.

Fischer, C. F., & King, R. M. (1995). *Authentic assessment: A guide to implementation.* Thousand Oaks, CA: Corwin Press.

Hart, D. (1994). *Authentic assessment: A handbook for educators.* Menlo Park, CA: Addison-Wesley.

Herman, J. L., Aschbacher, P. R., & Winters, L. (1992). *A practical guide to alternative assessment.* Alexandria, VA: Association for Supervision and Curriculum Development.

Marzano, R. J., Pickering, D., & McTighe, J. (1993). *Assessing student outcomes: Performance assessment using the dimensions of learning model.* Alexandria, VA: Association for Supervision and Curriculum Development.

McMillan, J. H. (1997). *Classroom assessment: Principles and practice for effective instruction.* Boston: Allyn & Bacon.

Pomperaug Regional School District 15 (1996). *A teacher's guide to performance-based learning and assessment.* Alexandria, VA: Association for Supervision and Curriculum Development.

Stiggins, R. J. (1997). *Student-centered classroom assessment* (2nd Ed.). New York: Macmillan College Publishing Company.

Wiggins, G. P. (1998). *Educative assessment: Designing assessments to inform and improve student performance.* San Francisco: Jossey-Bass.

There are also a number of video programs available that can provide quick but adequate coverage of the topic. An excellent list of videos can be found at the Maryland Assessment Consortium's Web site:

http://mac.cl.k12.md.us:2000/resources/videotape.html

It is not necessary to become an *expert* on the principles and practices of performance-based assessment in order to ensure the success of your parent and community involvement initiative. But it is important to understand how the current practices are alike and different from the practices used in the past. Most important, it is important to be able to *explain the differences* to parents and community members.

ENTHUSIASM

If schools promote parent and community involvement, it will happen. If they don't, it won't. Barclay and Boone have cited research that indicates a "critical factor in predicting the extent of parent involvement occurring in a school is the interest and initiative of the principal" (1996, p. 31). The principal is the person who can convince teachers that parent and community involvement programs can be designed so that they *help* teachers. He or she is also likely to have the most knowledge about the families of the children the school serves.

Enthusiasm, as we all know, is contagious. School and school system leaders who believe in, support, and actively promote performance-based assessment can exert remarkable influence on staff, students, parents, and the community. Where new initiatives are concerned, the real power of leadership is evident. Leaders should not underestimate the value of clear support and avid enthusiasm in ensuring the success of new efforts.

PERSISTENCE

Meeting resistance is one of the biggest challenges of leadership in times of change. How you approach it is the key. Resistance can be intense and tenacious in regard to performance-based assessment, and patient persistence is the only thing that can counteract it.

Adults seem to fall into two categories: Those who immediately love performance-based assessment and those who immediately and intensely hate it. The latter group is usually larger. People have been known to pass by a display of information on a new state performance assessment and make rude comments usually reserved for bars and football games. (No modeling of positive attitudes toward performance-based assessment in *those* homes!) Wisdom has evolved from dealing with such animosity. There are several things to keep in mind.

First, there are some people who will never accept performance-based assessment. They persist in thinking it is something new and subversive, and no amount of good sense and patience seems to sway their opinion. Accept it.

Second, remember that you are not just dealing with something new. You are dealing with fear and anxiety. You have to overcome the fear and anxiety before you can appeal to the intellect. People need to see exemplars and have the opportunity to ask questions about the *new* methods. They need to have the opportunity to vent their frustrations. Remember that if they don't vent their frustrations in front of you, they will vent them elsewhere, and you will have no opportunity to answer them. Although you may feel at times as if you need a bulletproof vest, or at least a shield against flying tomatoes, it will pay off in the long run if you persistently allow people to work out their fears, anxieties, and doubts. Performance-based assessment makes a lot of common sense, and eventually common sense will prevail. Most people eventually understand the value of performance-based assessment and come to accept it as an important part of a good education.

> **You have to overcome the fear and anxiety before you can appeal to the intellect.**

Third, remember that staff members are parents, too. They meet and talk to other parents on ball fields, in fast-food restaurants, in church, at karate lessons, on golf courses, and in grocery stores. Resistance from the *inside* may be one of your most serious problems, because it has the potential to intensify rather than curb the growth of resistance on the *outside*. Persistence is required in order to bring your entire staff around to acceptance and embracement of new ideas.

BACK-UP LEADERSHIP

Many excellent programs and initiatives have failed simply because the initiating leadership moves on. A change as important and influential as the emphasis on performance-based assessment needs back-up leadership to assure endurance. Assistant principals and others who may move into positions of leadership in the future need to be an integral part of the planning and implementation of any new program. Parent involvement is likely to be one of the first things to fall off if there is a significant leadership change in the middle of implementation, which could seriously hamper overall success in the long run. Therefore it is important for school leaders to train, support, and mentor alternate leaders. If you are lucky enough to have an assistant, give ample opportunity for the person to be involved *well enough* to become *invested* in the changes. Being *familiar* with them isn't enough. If you do not have an assistant, or even if you do, you should also consider the value of facilitating high involvement for teachers on your staff who have positions of leadership (e.g., department chairs) or who are natural leaders among the staff. Those who will take up the reins in the future must be as knowledgeable, enthusiastic, and persistent as you are, or the initiative will gradually become less important and eventually cease to exist.

> **A change as important and influential as the emphasis on performance-based assessment needs back-up leadership to assure endurance.**

THE IMPORTANCE OF CONSISTENCY

The differences in practice between what we used to do in assessment and what we do now are crucial. This is one of the major reasons why helping parents and the community understand performance-based assessment is so important. As a matter of course, when teachers and parents emphasize different skills and strategies for learning, they decrease the student's ability to generalize the skills required to achieve success. Students are effectively pulled back and forth from one orientation to another, with less opportunity for the activities of school and home to build upon one another. Some parents may actually use strategies that are detrimental. This can contribute to a decline in students' confidence. If, for instance, a parent is unwilling to appreciate the risk-taking of inventive spelling, the child's writing may be reduced to only those words for which they have memorized the conventional spelling. It is essential, therefore, for everyone participating in the student's education to be *on the same page*.

Parents and others who work with students outside of school need to be aware of how the new strategies differ from previous practice, they need to know why we are doing things differently, and they need to be given specific guidance on how to support what is happening in school. Your efforts need to include day care providers, tutoring services, psychologists in private practice, and anyone else who normally assists students with schoolwork.

WHERE TO BEGIN

Three things which are needed to ensure that the parent and community involvement component of any new initiative is effective were mentioned in the first chapter. They were (a) a clear understanding of the needs of the parent population, (b) appropriately budgeted time, and (c) the involvement of stakeholders.

GETTING STARTED

Principals and other school leaders normally have a clear understanding of the needs of the parent population, because they are customarily familiar with the personalities, attitudes, levels of education, occupations and other influencing factors of their students' parents. They are normally also familiar with the attitudes and capabilities of the school community in general. An articulation of how this translates into a plan of action for any new initiative is all that may be needed. If school leaders make it a point to talk candidly to parents and other members of the community about the new initiative and listen reflectively, invite parents and community members to be a part of the discussion surrounding the new initiative, and if the information learned is considered with care (objectively, not in a defensive mode) by school staff, the needs of the group will evolve easily. A formal needs assessment is rarely needed. The next step is to translate the needs revealed into a plan of action that is systematic and thorough, leaving no need unaddressed and providing appropriate coverage for all of them.

A brainstorming session with school staff during which you discuss and list parent opinions and needs should come first. Next match each need with a proposed activity. Group the activities in a logical manner and map out an overall approach that covers all of the needs in a thorough manner.

Where to Begin

♦ **Brainstorm with staff**

♦ **Match needs with activities**

♦ **Group activities**

♦ **Map out an approach**

Budgeting the time to implement an approach to parent and community education and involvement may be more difficult, because there is usually a point in time at which it is most effective to begin this effort. Doing it too soon as well as doing it too late can both be nonproductive. For instance, you cannot begin to implement a parent and community component before you have enough information yourself to answer questions with confidence. In addition, staff need to be able to articulate the concepts surrounding the initiative or they have the potential to be counterproductive in getting the message out. This situation, alone, can prove to be a highly significant influence on the overall success of your efforts. Materials have to be available to provide information when parents have additional questions, and for distribution to the community in general. The solution to this dilemma is to begin planning for the involvement of parents and the community immediately and simply to be ready when the opportunities present themselves.

Involving all stakeholders is a crucial element of the success of any new initiative, but this may be even more important when the initiative is as emotionally laden as changes in student assessment practices. In this case, involvement is educational. Those parents and community members who are involved in the new initiative from the beginning will be your first line of defense when it comes time to publicize the need for and the value of the new initiative. True, it will be necessary to spend a considerable amount of time familiarizing the participants with the principles surrounding the new initiative and gaining their understanding and acceptance of it, but time invested will pay off nicely in the long run. Stakeholders in general need to know that there are members of their constituency who support the changes and who believe that the changes will pay off in terms of a better educational experience for all students.

Remember that the business community is also a rich source of support. Epstein and Scott-Jones have remarked that the "...needs of business and industry and the goals of education are converging. Businesses need successful schools that produce students who are ready and able to work. [They] are coming to believe that it is better to support school programs for youngsters than to pay later to train or educate workers...."(1993, p. 6) Including businesses in your community involvement efforts is always a good idea, but in the case of new initiatives in the realm of performance-based assessment, businesses may be your greatest source of influence since their investment in the change may have significant payoffs for them in the future.

It may be useful to establish an advisory committee at the beginning to gain the interest, assistance and support of at least one representative of each constituent group. Such a committee could have as members a parent, a member of the business community, a higher education representative, a teacher, a central office employee, a classified employee, a representative of local civic groups, and any other individuals who would represent groups with a strong interest in the new initiative. Such community-based committees seem to work best when there is a fairly structured task to accomplish at each meeting. Tasks can include reviewing and synthesizing survey information, developing a list of target audiences and suggested agendas, reviewing and adapting print information, designing flyers and other handouts, recommending sources of support, recommending strategies for contacting participants, and recommending ways to publicize events.

Advisory Committee Tasks

♦ **Review survey information**

♦ **Develop list of targeted audiences**

♦ **Suggest agendas**

♦ **Review and adapt print information**

♦ **Design flyers**

♦ **Recommend sources of support**

♦ **Recommend contact strategies**

♦ **Recommend publicity strategies**

SETTING THE STAGE FOR UNDERSTANDING

Some adults are unable to conceptualize performance-based assessment due to the absence of cognitive links to this kind of learning. Many adults today think they do not have any experience with performance-based assessment. They only know what they experienced in school themselves, which was mostly selected-response assessment. To build cognitive links for understanding, present-day practice must be linked to something the adult knows, such as practices in the workplace. Humor helps a lot to ease the anxiety and help people understand the ideas. Use cartoons as often as you can when working with parents.

> **If you need an activity to help adults see the connections between performance-based assessment and the workplace, you may want to use the *Activity for Reflection on the Performance-Based Workplace* (Figure 2.2, p. 26) at the end of this chapter. Divide participants into groups of 3 or 4. Give them a copy of the worksheet and tell them they will have about 10 minutes to complete all 4 lists. When they are finished completing the lists, have a brief discussion about the efficiency of the various methods of assessment for each type of workplace skill, and draw some conclusions about the comparability of knowledge, reasoning, and skills that are taught in schools.**

For all of the activities outlined in this book, you should draw comparisons to the work world as often as you can. Begin with blue-collar jobs to make sure you do not imply that performance-based assessment is something that only applies to the professions. Ask people to think about what employers are telling us today, that motivates us to change the way we teach and assess students.

One thing employers are telling us is that workers need to be able to solve problems both independently and as part of a group. They need to be able to answer questions such as:

♦ Why did the tortillas come out orange instead of golden yellow?

♦ Why was the car's alignment worse when the car left the shop than it was when it came in?

♦ Why did the computer print the documents in reverse order?

♦ Why was there black pepper in the cinnamon when the jars of spice came off of the production line?

Sample overheads for these questions, which you may want to use during presentations to parent groups, are included at the end of this chapter (Figures 2.3 (p. 27), 2.4 (p. 28), 2.5 (p. 29), and 2.6 (p. 30)).

Most working adults tend to agree that today's workers need to be self-starting, independent thinkers who are able to adapt to the changing needs of the workplace by constantly relearning skills and realigning their thinking. These needs are the same no matter what type of work an individual does. We need to help parents and the community to understand that relying exclusively or almost exclusively on selected-response assessment does not promote the kind of critical, independent thinking that fosters relearning and realignment.

PARENT ROLES AS INSTRUCTORS

From the beginning, it is important to understand how parents and other members of the community differ in their prior knowledge and skill with regard to performance-based assessment. As you begin, you will face a wide range of acceptance and understanding of the principles and practices of performance-based assessment. You need to be prepared to meet the needs of several different groups and to make the most of your avenues of support in order to maximize your success.

There are three kinds of parent roles as instructors: Those who are experts, those who are competent, and those who are skilled if trained. (McGilp & Michael, 1994, pp. 21–22)

♦ The *experts* are usually professionally qualified and fluent in the knowledge and skills in which they instruct their children.

♦ Those who are *competent* often have well-developed skill in step-by-step instruction which arises from their interests and hobbies.

♦ Parents who attend training sessions at their children's school to learn skills that they subsequently teach to their children are the ones who are *skilled if trained*.

EXPERTS

Parents who are *experts* routinely demonstrate to their children a relationship between school learning and adult work. They can easily make the transition between skills learned in school and skills needed in the workplace or community. They frequently *already have* the knowledge and expertise we are trying to help our *teachers* learn, because they have adapted their professional lives to the needs of the workplace. They are a valuable resource to you as you try to prepare other parents and members of the community for changes in educational practice. They will be the first ones to understand the background and principles of performance-based assessment, and they will in most cases enthusiastically support the changes being implemented. They will be the ones who come up after the first presentation on performance-based methods and say that they can really relate to what was said because they see the trends you mentioned already occurring in their workplace. They may even say that they are relieved to see the changes coming! You will not need to provide much training for these parents and other community members. Solicit their support and include them as active participants in the process of instructional change.

COMPETENT INSTRUCTORS

Parents who are *competent* as instructors frequently have interests and/or hobbies which require the same kinds of skills as performance-based assessment. They know the importance of reading carefully to perform a task, following multistep instructions, completing tasks in an orderly manner and numerous other skills. They are able to translate their skills easily when the principles and practices of performance-based assessment are explained to them. They will benefit from frequent contact and follow-up in order to strengthen the skills that they learn. They are a valuable resource because they can model new skills for others from the perspective of being a *beginner*.

Both *expert* and *competent* parent instructors usually have a network of colleagues and fellow enthusiasts in the wider community, from whom their children also learn.

SKILLED IF TRAINED

The third category of parents as instructors, those who are *skilled if trained*, are the ones who most need the information and training that you will provide. They may be enthusiastic and eager to help their students, yet are not sure where to begin. Or, they may be less than enthusiastic, dubious about helping their students and somewhat unwilling to learn how. They will need help in understanding the background behind the new initiatives, the rationale for change, the differences between previous practice and current practice, and specific strategies that they can use to help their children be successful. They will have varying levels of motivation and willingness to learn, which means that a variety of formats and intensities will be required to meet their needs. They will also require more frequent contact and follow-up in order to maintain their skills. If you neglect this group, they are likely to assume the changes are no longer needed and may slip back into previous methods of helping their children.

Throughout the remainder of this book the needs and expectations of each of these groups will be pointed out at the beginning of appropriate chapters so that you can know what to expect from each group as you plan and implement your activities.

WHAT PARENTS AND THE COMMUNITY NEED TO KNOW

Aside from basic principles of performance-based techniques, what else do parents and members of the community need to know about this form of assessment? The answer is, as much as you can teach them. If they are to become your allies, they need to have a clear understanding of the theoretical basis for performance-based assessment as well as a well-developed set of implementation skills. The following is a list of six basic ideas that you may or may not want to use as the ground plan for your parent education activities. You may decide that some of these ideas are more or less appropriate for your situation. Feel free to use the ideas according to your needs.

What Parents and the Community Need to Know

1. **Selected-response assessment is not bad in and of itself, it is just not appropriate for every learning target and for every learning style.**

2. **Good assessment begins with good planning.**

3. **Performance-based assessment requires students to *demonstrate* what they know and can do, rather than *select* an answer from a given set of possibilities.**

4. **Teaching to the test has taken on a new meaning.**

5. **Studying for performance-based assessments is different from studying for selected-response tests.**

6. **Parent and community involvement makes a difference.**

SELECTED-RESPONSE ASSESSMENT IS NOT BAD IN AND OF ITSELF; IT IS JUST NOT APPROPRIATE FOR EVERY LEARNING TARGET OR FOR EVERY LEARNING STYLE

Selected-response assessment is like an old pair of shoes to many people. It has been around for a long time, it is comfortable, it is what we are used to. We know what to expect and how to prepare for it. Most adults today grew up with selected-response assessment as the main method of assessment used in schools, on standardized tests, on employment tests, and in college. It is the only way many people know and it is assumed to be the better way. After all, it has been used successfully for many years in many circumstances, and has performed well. Right?

One of the first things we need to help adults understand is that selected-response is *not an inappropriate way to assess* what learners have learned, it is just *not as appropriate* as other methods of assessment under certain circumstances. We need to match our method of assessment to our method of instruction and to our goals for instruction.

There are many examples related to life and to the work world that we can use to help adults understand this concept. They point out the need to know without a doubt that learners *can do what it is they are supposed to have learned how to do*. For instance, most adults would not want to ride in an airplane if they thought the pilot had demonstrated his ability to fly the plane by no other means than a selected-response test. They recognize that it is essential for that pilot to have taken some sort of test wherein it was necessary to actually fly the plane. Similarly, most adults would not want to pay a plumber to rework the plumbing in their house if the plumber had demonstrated his ability to perform the task using only a paper-and-pencil test. Many occupations require performance-based testing in order to ensure that the professionals can do what it is they have supposedly learned how to do.

Some Jobs That Require Performance-Based Certification				
teacher	surgeon	airplane pilot	plumber	carpenter
police officer	mechanic	firefighter	x-ray tech	chef
bus driver	typist	bricklayer	nurse	machinist

What is different about the learning of students in schools? Some things *can* be verified with selected-response assessment, such as the events of history and multiplication facts. But other things *cannot* be verified efficiently with this form of assessment. These other things, such as the ability to write a convincing persuasive letter, or the ability to set up a safe and effective experimental situation, or the ability to properly and safely use a saw, *must* be verified by asking the students to show us they can *do* them.

Additionally, selected-response assessment is not necessarily the most appropriate form of assessment for all student learning styles. Some students are not good selected-response test takers. They naturally prefer to demonstrate what they know by writing, speaking, performing, and other more active forms of assessment. These students are often the ones who get excellent grades in their classroom work, but get poor grades on tests, baffling their parents and teachers. The answer is often another form of assessment, one that allows the student to construct responses rather than selecting them. For these students, performance-based assessment is a more appropriate educational strategy.

GOOD ASSESSMENT BEGINS WITH GOOD PLANNING

Much hue and cry accompanied the resurgence of the term *outcome-based* a few years ago. I laughed about that, because I was required to use an outcome-based approach to my teaching when I began my career some 30 years ago.

Outcome-based teaching is simply what Steven Covey (1989) refers to as "beginning with the end in mind." You have to know what it is you want students to know and be able to do *before* you start teaching, so that you can teach them appropriately! If being certain about what it is you want students to know and be able to do is important, then it stands to reason you should also have some idea about how you are going to identify it when you see it. This is assessment. You ask yourself the question, "How am I going to be sure they know it (or can do it)?" You are planning the method of assessment you will use and, by so doing, you are using an outcome-based approach. This is not bad—it is good planning.

Most adults can relate to this concept because it makes sense that, in the world of work, it is not advisable to begin a project without first knowing what the objective is and how one will know when it is reached. Some form of performance evaluation is utilized in most jobs, so adults should be able to relate to the concept of *knowing how assessment is going to occur before work is begun.* How is the work going to be judged when it is completed? Who will be looking at it? How will they decide if the work is acceptable? What are the specific criteria on which the work will be judged? Will there be an opportunity to redo the work if it is not acceptable? These types of outcome-based questions form the basis of task structuring, and the answers allow workers to plan an approach that will result in maximum performance.

> **In the world of work, it is not advisable to begin a project without first knowing what the objective is and how one will know when it is reached.**

The difference between schools and the work place has been that, in schools, we haven't always articulated how we were going to assess skills, because it was assumed that it would be with a selected-response test. Now we are more precise in articulating how learning will be assessed, and teaching is planned accordingly.

PERFORMANCE-BASED ASSESSMENT REQUIRES STUDENTS TO DEMONSTRATE WHAT THEY KNOW AND CAN DO, RATHER THAN TO SELECT AN ANSWER FROM A GIVEN SET OF POSSIBILITIES

Although they have more than likely experienced performance-based assessment many times (I am fond of asking my students if they have ever taken a performance-based assessment and then surprising all those who answer "no" by assuming that they do not have a driver's license), most adults do not relate to this form of assessment. They are so accustomed to the word *test* meaning selected-response that they tend to ignore the fact that much of life involves actually demonstrating what one knows and can do rather than selecting a response from among several choices. This begins early in life, in art class, in music instruction, in scouting when badges are sought, and in swimming lessons, it continues through the formative school years in home arts and industrial arts classes, in sports, and in driver's education classes, and it culminates when young adults seek certification in a career field.

Educational assessment has traditionally meant selected-response, in spite of the fact that much of what is being taught involves performance types of learning goals. Adults need to understand that, in school as well as in real life, some behaviors can only be effectively evaluated by asking the learner to *demonstrate* mastery. It is not difficult for most adults to understand this when examples are pointed out and when they are given the opportunity to reflect on their past experiences.

If you want to show adults the difference between demonstrating what they know versus selecting an answer, share with them the following examples from two physics tests. Show the performance assessment item first, then show the traditional assessment item, after they have had an opportunity to think about the first item for a few minutes.

Performance Assessment Item

Driving to work, you are approaching a traffic light. Just beyond the traffic light is a steep incline. An 18-wheeled truck is stopped in the right lane at the light, and all of the other vehicles (cars and small trucks) are in the left lane. Using appropriate physics terms, explain why the other vehicles are all in the left lane.

Traditional Assessment Item

Driving to work, you are approaching a traffic light. Just beyond the traffic light is a steep incline. An 18-wheeled truck is stopped in the right lane at the light, and all of the other vehicles (cars and small trucks) are in the left lane. What is the most likely explanation for why all of the other vehicles are in the left lane?

1. They were all in the left lane in the first place.

2. They all intend to turn left at the next intersection.

3. Those who were in the right lane moved to the left lane because they know the truck will go slowly up the hill.

TEACHING TO THE TEST HAS TAKEN ON A NEW MEANING

Over the 60-some years that selected-response has been our chief method for assessment of student achievement, we have developed a disdainful attitude about test preparation. Many adults think of test preparation as cheating. Having done it themselves, they know that drilling and practicing creates an artificial result that is not a true indication of what the students know. Charges of *teaching to the test* often accompany the news that a certain school or school system has done well on standardized tests.

While it is true that drilling and practicing in isolation rarely creates enduring knowledge, and that performance-based assessment is no different than selected-response assessment in this sense, there is a very different concept operating when we refer to *teaching to the test* in relation to performance-based assessment. When teachers know what it is they expect students to know and be able to do, and when they know how they will recognize it when they see it (by having it demonstrated during a performance assessment), they can provide instruction that is highly goal-directed and efficient. They are, for all intents and purposes, *teaching to the test*. But that is *good*, because in order to demonstrate their learning in the context of the assessment, students have to have been given instruction that is similar in context.

Teachers have always felt it to be part of their responsibility to help students do their best on assessments, and therefore we teach test-taking skills in school. Test-taking skills are not *teaching to the test*. Teaching test-taking skills does not create an artificial result. Results remain an appropriate, true indication of what the students know. Test-taking skills allow students to overcome anxiety caused by their desire to do well and help them approach test taking in an organized and systematic manner.

**Test-Taking Skills Appropriate
for Performance-Based Tests**

♦ **Reading directions carefully and understanding what is being assessed and what kind of response is required.**

♦ **Planning out written answers using graphic organizers or acronyms.**

♦ **Knowing how to pace responses to complete all questions appropriately.**

♦ **Knowing when writing skills are being assessed and when they're not, and how to respond accordingly.**

♦ **Reviewing responses for thoroughness and accuracy.**

STUDYING FOR PERFORMANCE-BASED ASSESSMENTS IS DIFFERENT THAN STUDYING FOR SELECTED-RESPONSE TESTS

If parents are helping their children study the way they (the parents) learned to study for selected-response tests, they are drilling them and helping them memorize declarative knowledge. Remember the days when Friday morning's breakfast menu included reciting your spelling words one more time before the test? Today things are very different. Students need to be able to *demonstrate* what they know and can do, which means practice of a different sort. Spelling tests now require students to be able to use new words meaningfully, not just to recite them. Mathematics tests require students to be able to apply the math concepts to solving problems, not just to recite the facts.

For example, my students studied for the first performance-based assessment they had ever taken by memorizing formulas and going over definitions of terms—strategies that had worked well in the past. They were allowed to have a single piece of paper with notes during the test, so they wrote down all the formulas and definitions and were confident they would do well on the test. When they had to demonstrate what they knew and could do, however, they found that they should have *practiced* using the formulas and should have *thought about* the concepts and principles they were learning rather than just memorized the definitions. Why? Because it took more than half of the allocated exam time to *figure out* how to carry out the formulas, and there were no questions about definitions on the test!

Study Techniques for Performance-Based Tests

♦ **Practice processes and procedures.**

♦ **Generate possible questions (based on the stated learning goals) and write out possible answers.**

♦ **Review handouts and notes, and make study notes. Categorize such things as dates, events, important persons, and key terms.**

♦ **Look for connections among key concepts.**

PARENT AND COMMUNITY INVOLVEMENT HELPS

Everything you read about school and family connections these days says the same thing about the value of parents helping their children with their studies. Research shows that parent involvement improves student achievement, attitudes, homework, report card grades, and aspirations (Epstein, 1992). The benefits are clear. When parents give appropriate help at home, achievement is enhanced. Extra learning time at home can actually produce gains in early elementary students' reading scores that are equal to gains made by students who participate in *pull-out* programs in school. (Epstein, 1990, p. 111) This is a profound statement when considered in terms of the cost of *pull-out* programs in today's schools. One could feasibly say that consistent, appropriate assistance at home could save school systems millions of dollars each year and allow some students to participate more inclusively in the learning opportunities offered by classroom teachers.

GETTING YOUR MESSAGE ACROSS

When parents are asked about their contacts with schools, they generally don't say they prefer a business-like and professional manner. They prefer a more comfortable, friendly touch that emphasizes personal attention and timely information (Jones, 1991, p. 17). The procedures outlined in the pages that follow are based upon an approach that is collaborative, congenial, and flexible. Parents are treated like partners, presentations are less structured and non-threatening, and the overall program changes to meet the needs of those it serves. The reason this is so important in this case goes back to the existence of fear and anxiety regarding tests. You cannot expect people who feel threatened in the first place to respond to new ideas unless they feel accepted, comfortable, and unhurried.

Personal contacts should be discretionary and low-key. Written communication should be clear, brief, respectful, and free from educational jargon. Emotion-laden reactions should be treated with acceptance and not defensiveness. Experience has shown that if you try to convince an adult that performance-based assessment is the best thing since sliced bread when they clearly have an aversion to it, you will cause them to be *less* willing to consider it as a reasonable approach. It is better to accept their point of view and hope that the tide of change will eventually sweep them along.

ROADBLOCKS TO SUCCESS

Aside from the potential difficulties related to fear of tests mentioned earlier, there are several other roadblocks that you may face.

One of these is willingness to participate in parent training activities. Research has shown that over 90% of *all* parents of elementary and middle school students believe the school should tell them how to help at home. Eighty-five percent would help out more if they knew how (Epstein, 1990, p. 107). But few parents ever show up when we offer training activities at school.

It may be difficult to entice some parents into actually doing what they seem to be willing to do, but persistence can pay off. Sometimes this means going to them rather than expecting them to come to you. Schools have reported good results by taking their parent training efforts off-campus to places like churches or community centers. Others have gone totally public with practices such as providing bits of information and hints for helping students with homework on place mats at the local fast-food restaurants. Knowing your community is an important factor in your success in this regard. If you find out where the parents and other community members *are*, you will know where to reach them.

Another potential roadblock may arise if your staff does not completely understand what performance-based assessment requires of students in terms of non-academic skills. It is not always a lack of knowledge or understanding that prevents students from doing their best on performance-based assessments. It can often be a matter of poor motivation, lack of self-confidence, poor study habits, or ineffective approaches to problem solving. Students in one school system who, on a state-mandated performance-based assessment, came close to satisfactory performance but did not quite reach it, were found to be those who were not persistent, could not work independently, were not organized in their work habits, and did not know how to pace themselves through highly scaffolded tasks. Teachers and other staff need to be aware of these associated skills so that they can encourage parents to focus on them at home. Parents who do not fully understand what performance-based assessment is and how it translates into instructional strategies can still support it by focusing on the associated skills and by encouraging good attitudes about it in their children. They can help motivate their children to do well.

PARTING WORDS ON STAFF INVOLVEMENT

Epstein (1986) has reported that in a survey of 1,269 students in Maryland schools, about 58% of the parents *rarely* or *never* received requests from their child's teacher to become involved in learning activities at home. Fewer than 30% of them said that they were given many ideas about how to help their child with schoolwork. Many of these parents felt that they should only help their child if the *teacher* asked them to. Other sources of requests (e.g., newsletters) did not make them think that their help was necessary.

This information points out the importance of your staff development activities in aiding your parent and community involvement efforts. Teachers need to be aware of their importance in the overall success of the school's parent involvement efforts. They need to understand the reasons why the program should prove to be beneficial, how successful involvement programs operate, and how they can take action to ensure the success of the school's efforts. Many or most of your staff will need to learn these things through carefully planned staff development, because they are not customarily taught in teacher preparation programs.

FIGURE 2.2 ACTIVITY FOR REFLECTION ON
THE PERFORMANCE-BASED WORKPLACE

List some of the little bits of information you have to *know* in order to do your job.

If your boss wanted to assess your knowledge of this information, you could take a multiple-choice test.

List some of the things you have to be able to *decide* in order to do your job.

If your boss wanted to see if you could think out one of these decisions, you could take an essay test.

List some of the *skills* you have to be able to do in order to do your job.

If your boss wanted to know if you could adequately do these things, you would have to take a performance assessment.

List some of the things you need to be able to *produce* in order to do your job.

If your boss wanted to know if you could adequately produce these things, you would have to take a performance assessment.

FIGURE 2.3 OVERHEAD 1—TORTILLAS

Why did the tortillas come out orange instead of golden yellow?

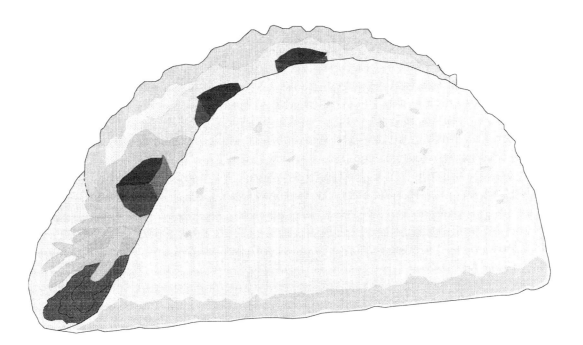

FIGURE 2.4 OVERHEAD 2 — CAR ALIGNMENT

Why was the car's alignment worse when the car left the shop than it was when it came in?

FIGURE 2.5 OVERHEAD 3 — PRINT IN REVERSE

Why did the computer print the documents in reverse order?

FIGURE 2.6 OVERHEAD 4 — BLACK PEPPER

Why was there black pepper in the cinnamon when the jars of spice came off of the production line?

3

STEP ONE: INTRODUCING PERFORMANCE-BASED ASSESSMENT

It's probably clear from Chapter 2 that this book recommends doing a great deal of *advance work* before you begin working directly with parents and the community to develop their understanding of performance-based assessment. The process recommended probably seems extended and pieced out. The best argument for completing the process step-by-step, however, is that it works! We start with what we call a *drive-by introduction*.

WHAT TO DO

There are two goals for Step One: Introduce the new idea to as many people as possible, and provide take-home information for those who accept the change intuitively and want to go on immediately to the next step.

You may also need to include a third goal if introduction of the new idea has already occurred through news releases and word-of-mouth. As is frequently the case, some of this information may have been erroneous, alarming, and/or presented in a confrontational manner. Therefore part of your purpose in the beginning may be to correct erroneous information, calm those who may be alarmed, and diffuse any confrontational situations that may have developed.

PARENT ROLES AS INSTRUCTORS

Parents who can be characterized as *experts* will probably understand the implications of the information instantly and may immediately and intuitively change the strategies they use when helping their children. Don't be surprised if they have few questions and do not *stick around* very long for the activities you have planned. It's not because they aren't interested. To the contrary, they may be very interested, just not so much that they want to *brave the crowd* at this particular point in time. Once you have introduced the idea of performance-based assessment publicly, these individuals often wait for an opportunity to get additional information on an individual basis. It does not take a lot of time to provide what they need, and they are usually quite willing to wait for it if you need to take time to pull it together. It's easy to forget to do so, however. You will need to be vigilant about recognizing these individuals. They have a tendency to melt into the crowd or to do what they see needs to be done on their own, and it is better to have them actively involved in the change process because they can be your strongest supporters.

Parents who are *competent* instructors will sense some familiarity with the concepts and may be intrigued by the apparent implications. They are likely to be eager for more information. They will be the ones who have numerous questions and will want you to repeat information a few times until they are comfortable with the connections that may seem too obvious to them. These individuals will probably make up a large part of your audience at your first group presentation. Be careful in trying to pick them out of the group. They can help you most by serving as models and helpers for the last group, those who are *skilled if trained*.

This last group of parents (*skilled if trained*) will be, of course, your greatest challenge. They may initially experience some anxiety when presented with the possibility that the practices they have worked hard to learn and apply consistently are no longer up-to-date. Understandably, they are probably very comfortable with strategies that have worked for generations. They may feel some sense of urgency to relearn how to best help their children. You may sense this urgency in the number of questions they ask and in the nature of the questions. You may encounter some doubt about the utility of the strategies you want them to learn, and possibly about the techniques (performance-based assessment) in general. You may need to be prepared to immediately inform this group when they will have their first opportunity to become familiar with the new ideas. Uncertainty may arouse anxiety, which may lead to negativity. For this reason you need to already have plans for the next step in the process, when you provide Step One activities.

INTRODUCE THE IDEA TO AS MANY PEOPLE AS POSSIBLE

When there are *many* people in a community who have accurate, trustworthy information about a new initiative, it is less likely that negative, biased attitudes will develop. It is in your best interests to get the word out to as many people as you can as soon as you can. This can be risky, because at the beginning of a new initiative we are not always sure of the accuracy of our information and understandably do not want to pass on information that we will have to revise or retract at a later date. Recently this has been a very real dilemma in many states during development of new statewide assessment programs. Information tends to be unreliable in the beginning, and that creates a problem for those who want to keep parents and the public informed. Educators are supposed to be accurate! We therefore must try to balance the need to get information out with the need to be confident that the information we are giving is going to remain accurate.

During this first step in the process you should be providing a minimum amount of information, and it might possibly come from a source outside of your school or school system. There are numerous sources from which you can access general information on performance-based assessment, so you do not have to be restricted to specific information about new policies and/or new assessments to accomplish the goal of introducing your target audience to the concepts. Remember that your goal is to get as *many* people as possible in possession of accurate, trustworthy information. Figure 3.1 (p. 34) is a list of Web sites that can be helpful in this regard.

PROVIDE TAKE-HOME INFORMATION

Although the main purpose of the first step is to introduce ideas to the target audience, you should not miss the opportunity to provide print information to those who want it or may be ready immediately to learn more about the new initiative. The information you provide should go slightly beyond the information offered in the initial presentation, but should not be overwhelming.

Remember also that you need to be very careful not to *fan the fire* in the case of individuals who are extremely negative about the initiative. Try to design the handouts so that they contain nothing that is controversial. If you can't avoid controversial material, present the facts as neutrally as you can.

CORRECT, CALM, AND DIFFUSE

Remembering that the subject of performance-based assessment can be highly-charged, and that information provided to the public in newspapers and other media reports is not always completely accurate or well-interpreted, you may be in the position of having to correct misinformation, face misjudgments and deal with intensely negative opinions. You may also need to calm people who are highly emotional about the changes, and to diffuse rumors.

It is not at all surprising that some people may come to your presentations angry or resentful, especially if they perceive that the actions being taken to change procedures are somehow biased or inequitable to one group or another. Be prepared for this from the very beginning of your efforts. It is *never* useful to

---

FIGURE 3.1 USEFUL WEB SITES

- Appalachia Regional Educational Laboratory: *http://www.ael.org*

- ERIC Clearinghouse on Assessment and Evaluation: *http://ericae.net*

- Family Education Network: *http://familyeducation.com*

- Family Involvement Partnership for Learning: *http://pfie.ed.gov*

- International Reading Association: *www.reading.org*

- National Association of Test Directors: *www.natd.org*

- National Center for Community Education: *http://www.nccenet.org/*

- National Center for Research on Evaluation, Standards, and Student Testing: *http://cresst96.cse.ucla.edu/index.htm*

- National Coalition for Parent Involvement in Education: *http://www.ncpie.org*

- National Council on Measurement in Education: *www.assessment.iupui.edu/NCME/NCME.html*

- National Parent Information Network: *http://npin.org/*

- National Parenting Center: *http://www.tnpc.com*

- National PTA: *www.pta.org/index.stm*

- National School Public Relations Association: *www.nspra.org/entry.htm*

- Parent Talk Newsletter: *http://www.tnpc.com/parentalk/index.html*

- Parenthood Web: *http://www.parenthoodweb.com*

- Parents Place: *http://www.parentsplace.com*

- Partnership for Family Involvement in Education (PFIE): *http://www.ed.gov*

- The Parent Institute: *www.parent-institute.com/*

---

be confrontational in responding to individuals who are negative about performance-based assessment. It is much better to expect some negativism, to be prepared to listen to what people have to say, to show people that you understand that they have negative feelings, and to have concise and non-defensive responses prepared in the event they are welcomed.

HOW TO DO IT

The first step in any process is often the most critical, especially when you are dealing with something that engenders either fear or highly emotional opinions. Assessment does both. Therefore, to assure the success of the change you are trying to implement, the first step should be orchestrated in such a way as to help alleviate the fear and allow for those who have strong opinions to express them in a constructive way.

The best way to take the first step in introducing parents and other members of the community to performance-based assessment is to do it in an informal manner. This is called the *drive-by* step. Make information available so that those who are interested can get it, but do not subject an entire audience to a presentation format. Provide a knowledgeable individual who can answer questions and provide additional information if people want it. This strategy serves several purposes.

First, it gives the target audience an opportunity to choose whether or not they wish to receive information. This is empowering to those who are fearful. It is also perceived as thoughtful since those who wish to receive information can do so without having to sit through a long program which may contain much more information than they are currently ready to receive and process. They can take the information, return home with it, read it and process it at their own pace. They can then seek more information when they are ready for it.

Secondly, it gives those who have highly emotional opinions the opportunity to confront the issues in a small, one-on-one forum instead of in a large group where their opinions may serve to fuel the undeveloped opinions of others. It allows school personnel an opportunity to just listen rather than having to react to strong opinions, which is expected when the opinions are expressed in a large-group setting. When you are the presenter of a more *formal* program and someone expresses a strong opinion (usually during the question and answer period), you must respond to the concern or appear to be avoiding questions. In an *informal* setting, however, you can employ active listening and give the person with the opinion an opportunity to vent. This alone can prove to be an extremely valuable strategy in efforts to change public opinion about the methods used to assess students.

Third, this strategy allows the presentation of information as it is being received, early in the change process. It is easier to present a small amount of information in an informal setting where the same amount of information would not justify a more formal meeting. It is also easier and more socially acceptable to say (honestly), "I don't know any more about the specifics of this process just yet" to a small group of people clustered around a display than it is to say the same thing to a large group called together specifically for a presentation.

Remember that your audience is made up of three kinds of parents as teachers: Those who are experts, those who are competent, and those who are competent when trained. Each group probably needs a different approach, so you should try to accommodate everyone's needs.

MAKE INFORMATION AVAILABLE

A display board that contains a summary of important information is an excellent means for achieving the goals of Step one. You can control the amount of information you want to dispense and can also present it concisely, logically, and appealingly.

Present only the main ideas you want to get across. For instance, the display we use covers only three ideas:

1. Traditional testing allows students to show mastery by memorizing and guessing;
2. Performance-based assessment requires students to use reasoning and application skills; and,
3. The result of using performance-based assessment is useful information about what the student knows and can do.

The parts of a performance-based assessment task are briefly outlined with simple headings: Read for Understanding, Use Tools, Solve Problems, and Respond Thoughtfully. Anyone who walks by the display and stops for a couple of minutes is able to grasp the main idea. If the idea intrigues them, they can spend more time and either talk to the individual standing by the display or take some of the information provided. They will also feel less threatened if there are fewer ideas to process.

Present the ideas in a logical sequence such as what used to be, why it is no longer the only useful method, how the new method is different, and what it gives us that the older method doesn't offer.

The more visually appealing your display is, the more positive feelings it will generate. You can do a lot toward counteracting negative attitudes with an appealing, child-centered display.

PROVIDE A KNOWLEDGEABLE INDIVIDUAL

Parents who are experts as well as those who are competent instructors may want or need immediate answers to questions generated by the information in your display. Others may need clarification of the information in order to make sure they understand it. You don't want the display to have the effect of confusing already hesitant or antagonistic individuals. Therefore it is wise to have a knowledgeable individual near the display who can answer questions, clarify information, and point people in the right direction if more information is needed.

The individual who is responsible for being available to talk to those who stop by the display and ask questions must obviously be knowledgeable about the testing program and about performance-based learning. This person must also be someone who can listen effectively and avoid becoming involved in confrontational exchanges about the *goodness* or *badness* of assessment methodology.

First meetings with the public regarding performance-based assessment can be quite disturbing at times and even confrontational. People seem to have very strong opinions about the issues and may not hesitate to express those opinions vociferously in public, especially if your efforts to give them information have been precipitated by the implementation of a new state or local mandated test. After having several meetings and informational presentations interrupted (at the least) and hijacked (at the worst) by individuals whose purpose in attending was to argue the efficacy of the methodology, we developed some dependable responses that we employed as soon as it became obvious that there was going to be a problem.

Remembering that most people hate tests and that many people are afraid of them, we felt it was important to be very careful not to sound condescending and to make sure people knew that we valued their opinions, even if those opinions did not agree with our own. The main point we tried to get across with our comments was that the purpose of the display or activity was to provide information to parents and the public, not to debate the efficacy of the methodology, but that we would be happy at some other time to listen to opinions and pass them along to the individuals who were making the decisions. We always tried to make sure that the individual manning the display at the initial steps of the parent and community educational process was prepared to respond in this way.

PROVIDE ADDITIONAL INFORMATION

Information provided at this step of the process should be simple and straightforward, and should anticipate questions adults would ask given their brief introduction to the ideas.

We always have examples available of the types of tasks found on the new assessments and also try to have examples of classroom tasks that are supportive of the assessments. In addition, we provide take-home information in the form of brief pamphlets or information sheets that are either designed by us or provided by the State Department of Education. If you design your own materials, try to limit information to single sheets of paper that reiterate the concepts presented in the display. It's a good idea to include a source of additional information, either a phone number, mailing address or web address. Several reprints that could be used or adapted for this purpose are included at the end of the chapter as Figures 3.2 (p. 39), 3.3 (p. 41), 3.4 (p. 43), and 3.5 (p. 45).

WHEN TO DO IT

Anyone who has ever tried to get parents and members of the community into a school to receive information knows that it can be an extremely frustrating experience, no matter how important the information is or how hard we try to entice the audience. There are a few times during any school year, however, when parents flock to schools and when community members are a *captive* audience. Fall open houses and holiday programs are the best examples of the former. Fairs, parades, grand openings, holiday sales, and concerts are good examples of the latter. In the case of middle schools and high schools, school sports events are also good opportunities to casually introduce new information and to put print materials in the hands of your target audience.

If your school system provides after-school day care, consider leaving a display in the day care area for a short period of time.

The ideal time to begin this effort is the beginning of the school year when you have access to the most participants in one place at one time. True, you probably cannot distract parents too much from their main motivation on these occasions, which is to meet the new teacher, see the new classroom, become oriented to the new school, and so forth. However, you can use these occasions to plant ideas, and to entice participation in other events.

Ideally, you should implement Step One at a point in time that permits implementation of the subsequent steps in the process sufficiently in advance of the administration of the test (if it is a state or local test). To have even minimum opportunity for impact on the students' performance, this probably means you should begin at least six months prior to the test.

FIGURE 3.3 MARYLAND SCHOOL PERFORMANCE ASSESSMENT PROGRAM

1. What is the Maryland School Performance Assessment Program (MSPAP)?

MSPAP is an assessment or testing program whose primary purpose is to provide information that can be used to improve instruction in schools. The MSPAP measures the performance of Maryland schools by illustrating:

- ❖ how well students solve problems cooperatively and individually
- ❖ how well students apply what they have learned to real world problems
- ❖ how well students can relate and use knowledge from different subject areas

2. How does the MSPAP differ from traditional achievement tests?

- ❖ MSPAP is intended to measure school improvement, not individual student performance.
- ❖ MSPAP tasks include a series of related steps that draw on knowledge across content areas.
- ❖ MSPAP tasks are related to "real-life" situations.
- ❖ MSPAP tasks typically require students to write extensively; they are not multiple choice questions that can be answered by simple rote learning and memorization of facts.

For example, one 5th grade task asks the student to figure out if the school can raise $200 for a school banner in a 6-week time frame. Using a chart on aluminium can recycling and responding to a number of specific questions, the student figures out the conditions necessary to reach the fund-raising goal, then writes a brief feasibility statement to present to the student council.

3. How many children participate in the MSPAP?

The MSPAP is administered to 3rd, 5th, and 8th grade students in the late spring. In 1998, approximately 181,781 students participated.

4. How was the MSPAP developed?

In May 1990, the State Board of Education approved student learning goals for the year 2000. An accountability system was needed to assess progress toward achievement of these learning outcomes. MSPAP is that accountability system. Development of the MSPAP has been a collaborative effort involving teachers and administrators throughout Maryland, curriculum and testing experts at the State Department of Education, and consultants whose specialty is test development. The process of designing and field testing MSPAP performance tasks and methods of scoring student answers has been a multi-year process.

5. How are MSPAP results reported?

In each content area, MSPAP results are reported through five proficiency levels, with level 1 being the most proficient. Proposed performance standards for schools and local systems to meet:

❖ Satisfactory — 70% of students scoring at proficiency level 3 or above

❖ Excellent — 70% of students scoring at level 3 or above, with at least 25% of students at level 2 or higher

6. Is individual student data available?

In order to keep MSPAP administration time to a minimum, each student is given only a portion of the assessment. Consequently, a complete MSPAP score does not exist for an individual student. This sampling technique does, however, provide the needed performance assessment information at the school, system, and state levels. School systems will make student test results available to parents, but student MSPAP data are useful only in context with all the measures and observations available for an individual child.

7. How is the MSPAP scored?

Student responses to the performance tasks are open-ended. A wide range of responses to each is acceptable. Some responses receive full credit, some partial credit, and some no credit, depending on the quality of the response. Responses to the MSPAP tasks are scored by teams of Maryland educators who have been specially trained to use scoring guidelines (called rules and rubrics).

8. Why has Maryland not yet met any of the proposed MSPAP standards?

The MSPAP measures the high quality application of knowledge that involves problem solving, decision making, and reasoning skills. The rigorous content of the tests relates to learning outcomes that have been established by the State Board of Education for the year 2000. School Improvement Teams in each public school in Maryland are working to adjust curriculum content and delivery to meet these goals.

**FIGURE 3.4 MSPAP THROUGH THE
EYES OF A 5TH GRADE STUDENT**

How might a Maryland School Performance assessment item--or task--be described by a student taking the MSPAP? Here is how the steps in a task on "Salinity" might be viewed by a 5th grader.

1. The teacher sets the stage

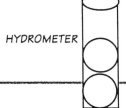

HYDROMETER

❖ My teacher tells us how important water is to life on planet earth and how the differences in the amount of salt (salinity) in the water affect the kinds of life that can exist in certain places. So we can understand salinity better, my teacher gives us the tools my classmates and I need to construct a hydrometer, a device that measures the amount of salt in the water. We do this using a drinking straw cut in half with one end sealed with clay and two BBs at the bottom to weight it down. We also get rulers, pen, tape, salt, and fresh water in cups from the teacher. As we start to work, she writes on the board how much time we have to complete each part of our task.

---

2. Then we work in groups

❖ Next, my classmates and I work together in a group, using our newly fashioned hydrometer to test two samples of water, one fresh and one salty. When we place the hydrometer in the fresh water, the teacher asks us to observe what occurs and then each of us draws a picture of what we see. Then we do the same thing when we put the hydrometer in the salt water.

❖ Now we are asked to decide what is the best way to measure the differences between the ways the hydrometer acts in different types of water. Once we have agreed on a method, we each write a description of how to measure.

---

3. We gather more information

❖ We then put the hydrometer in fresh water and salt water samples again. Only this time, instead of drawing a picture, we use our group's way of measuring the results and write these down instead. Then our teacher asks each of us to describe the difference between the two measurements and try to come up with possible explanations for the differences our group has observed between salt and fresh water. We write all these down in the space provided in our test booklets.

---

4. I put what I know to work

❖ Now, I try to predict the future. What do I think will happen when equal amounts of salt water and fresh water are mixed? How will the hydrometer react to this "brackish" water? The teacher asks each of us to make predictions, and for every prediction I make, I have to come up with a reason.

❖ It's time to put the predictions to the test. Working together, the teacher asks us to mix equal amounts of salt and fresh water, then test the mixture with the hydrometer. We record what happens. Did this investigation cause me to either accept or reject my predictions? Using evidence from the investigation, each of us must explain whether it did or not.

5. I use what I know to solve a problem

❖ Now our teacher explains that, in science, the salinity of water is measured in parts per thousand or "ppt." Certain types of water animals can only live in water that has the proper salinity level. We work individually, using a chart listing some examples of these creatures and the range of salinity "ppt" in which they can thrive. We also use a copy of a real salinity map of the Chesapeake Bay. The test booklet explains that the saltwater aquarium in our school has a salinity of between 16 and 30 ppt. Based on the information on the chart, we are asked which creatures would not be able to thrive in our aquarium, and which creatures require a lesser or greater salinity. Next, using the salinity map of the Chesapeake Bay, I must determine in which areas of the Chesapeake each animal might live. Now the whole idea of salinity makes a little more sense and is connected to the natural world.

SALINITY SURVIVAL ZONES

ORGANISM	SALINITY RANGE	ZONES WHERE THE ORGANISM CAN BE FOUND
Blue Crab	0-30 ppt	
Black Sea Bass	15-30 ppt	
Sea Nettle	7-30 ppt	
White Crappie	0 ppt	
Striped Bass	0-30 ppt	
Common Sea Star	18-30 ppt	
Marsh Periwinkle	0-15 ppt	
Waterweed	0-9 ppt	
Yellow Pond Lily	0 ppt	

❖ My final assignment is to write a paragraph describing how I would use a hydrometer so that, if our class went on a field trip and caught some small sea bass, we could make sure that the salinity in our aquarium would be right for our fish. The instructions in the test booklet tell me that I should write carefully and proofread my work.

**FIGURE 3.5 MSPAP THROUGH THE
EYES OF A 3RD GRADE STUDENT**

---

*How might a Maryland School Performance assessment item--or task--be
described by a student taking the MSPAP? Here is how the steps in a
task on "Planning a Zoo" might be viewed by a 3rd grader.*

**1. The teacher
gives us
floor plans.**

❖ My teacher says we're going to imagine that some people planning a new zoo in
our town have asked our class to help. In our activity papers, there are pictures of
three floor plans for three different animals in our zoo - a giraffe, a polar bear, and
an elephant. The key says that each little square on the plan is equal to one
square foot of real space. Next, we have to build a fence around each cage and
figure out how much it will cost. Fencing costs $8.00 per foot, so we have to
count each side of a square going around the cage. Once we find this number, it's
easy to multiply it by 8 on our calculators to find out how much putting a fence
around each cage will cost.

Floor Plan

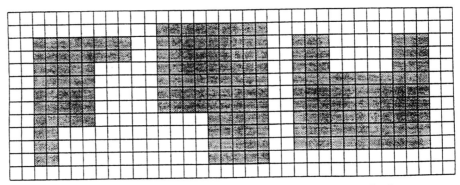

Cage A: Giraffe   Cage B: Polar Bear   Cage C: Elephant

Key: 1 ☐ = 1 square foot

2. More measuring and multiplying.

❖ Now we have to put some flooring in the cages to make the animals more comfortable. Each square foot of flooring costs $4.00. We have to figure out how much the flooring for each cage will cost. The easy way is just to count the squares. Then we multiply that number by 4 to find out how much it will cost to put a floor in each cage.

CAGE	AREA	COST
A		$
B		$
C		$

3. Each animal has special needs.

❖ The giraffe needs a square feed box measuring 4 square feet, and it has to be placed in the cage so the animal can get around it on all sides. I draw a box around four squares in the cage. Since the box isn't touching any walls, the giraffe will be able to move around it on all sides. The polar bear needs a swimming pool with a perimeter of twelve feet, and the pool should be in a corner of the cage. I draw a figure against one of the corners of the cage, making sure that the perimeter equals 12. The elephant needs two trees. The elephant is easy to please. I just draw two boxes that have the same size and shape.

CAGE	PERIMETER	COST
A		$
B		$
C		$

4. Creating a tile pattern.

❖ Our zoo will have an information office, and since we want everything to look nice, we have to make up a repeating pattern for the tiles on the floor of the office. I remember the pattern of our tiles in the kitchen at home. They look like a checkerboard. So I color in every other box in the rows of squares until it looks like our kitchen at home. I write a sentence about how I came up with the pattern.

❖ Then we're finished. Everybody had a lot of fun planning our zoo. It doesn't seem so hard now to plan something like a zoo, or maybe something else, like a bridge or a building. I bet that's not as hard as it looks either.

FIGURE 3.6 MSPAP THROUGH THE EYES OF AN 8TH GRADE STUDENT

How might a Maryland School Performance assessment item--or task--be described by a student taking the MSPAP? Here is how a task on "Planetary Patterns" might be viewed by an 8th grader.

1. **Exploring a new solar system.**

❖ Today, my teacher asked us to imagine that we were scientists working at the Goddard Space Flight Center in Greenbelt, Maryland. The *Voyager* spacecraft has been sending back data on a newly discovered solar system. There are four planets in this new system, and they have nearly circular orbits that do not overlap. A chart tells us the surface temperature, number of moons, tilt of axis and chemical composition of each planet. Based on this data and an orbit diagram, we have to identify similarities between patterns present in this new solar system and our own solar system. Looking at the model provided, I see that the planets in the new solar system orbit around a sun which is at the center of the system, just like ours. I also notice that the surface temperature of any planet in the system decreases as its distance from the sun increases.

2. **More questions, more patterns.**

❖ Next we are asked to come up with at least three questions about the new solar system which are not answered by the chart. I have quite a few questions about the system, including the size of each planet, each planet's distance from the sun, the atmospheric pressure of each planet, and the age of the planet. Next, I am asked to identify and write about three repeating patterns of astronomical change that occur in the sky. I remember that the moon goes through phases regularly, the sun rises and sets each day, and there is a difference in the position of the stars in the sky as the seasons change.

3. **Completing the orbit data logs and predicting planet positions.**

❖ My classmates and I are given a chart listing the position of the four planets in the new solar system for the months of January, February, March and April. Working with three other students, we must complete the orbit data logs, also provided in our packet, to show in a picture form where each planet is at each of these times. Working carefully, we pinpoint the position of each planet in each of the four months using the data given. Then, on our own, we use what we have learned about the rate of the orbit of each planet to predict the position of all four planets in the month of May. We are allowed to use pennies on our chart to represent planets and move them around the diagram to help make our predictions. Once our predictions are made, we write about our methods. I figured out how far each planet moved around its orbit in a month and moved the penny representing each planet the right distance, and there it was, at the right spot.

4. Reserving time on the orbiting space telescope.

❖ The next instructions I read ask me to imagine that *Space and Telescope Magazine* wants to record the next planetary alignment of this new solar system. To do this, I need to figure out when the planets will be aligned so I can reserve time on the orbiting space telescope. This takes a little more doing than the last task, and I find that using the pennies on my diagram helps me keep track of the motion of the planets. Carefully keeping track of which month I am in, I move each planet around its orbit the right number of spaces. Finally, after moving all the planets around their orbits several times, I come to a month when they are all in a row, or aligned. This is the month I predict should be reserved for the use of the orbiting space telescope.

5. Conclusions and explanations for younger students.

❖ Next, I write about how predicting the alignment of the planets was different from predicting their position in the month of May, one month after our data ended. It was a little more difficult to predict the alignment, but I found that by moving the pennies around the diagram one at a time and keeping track of the month, I was able to find the answer. In the space on our worksheet I write a paragraph for a younger student describing how the model of the solar system using orbit diagrams and pennies helped with my predictions. Finally, I write about how working with others in a group influenced or changed our beginning ideas about the position of the planets. My group basically agreed on how to go about predicting the positions of the planets, and our idea worked.

6. When we put it to the test, it was confirmed.

❖ Planetary Patterns was challenging, I had to think carefully and logically. I also got a chance to use information I learned in my science class.

4

STEP TWO: SHARING KNOWLEDGE ABOUT PERFORMANCE-BASED ASSESSMENT

During this step in the process of developing parent and community understanding of performance-based assessment, you will make your first attempt to provide information to *all* members of your target group. Yet you are still not at the point of conducting traditional workshops. There are several reasons for this, the most influential of which is that parents are customarily somewhat unresponsive to workshops. They are likely to be even less responsive when the topic is tests.

WHAT TO DO

After introducing the ideas in an informal way at Step One, your goals for Step Two will be to provide more detailed information, to establish background for the new methods, and to *begin* to teach strategies for helping students with homework and other performance-based schoolwork. You will do the teaching in a way that is not perceived by parents to be a traditional workshop, but instead is an informational opportunity to learn what their children are doing in school and how they can help them do it better.

PARENT ROLES AS INSTRUCTORS

Once again, parents who are *experts* may have understood the new ideas with little or no questions the first time they were exposed to them, and may have implemented changes in the strategies they use in helping their children without further assistance. They may actually not need additional information or organized training, so do not be disappointed if they politely decline to attend. It wouldn't hurt to seek them out when you have the chance and ask them if they had any questions about the new ideas. You could also encourage them to attend the family activity simply to show support for the new initiative, and also to help provide guidance for parents who are new to the techniques.

Those who are *competent* will understand the information you send home but will probably have some questions. They will come to family activities prepared to learn new techniques and eager to implement appropriate strategies to help their children.

Parents who are *skilled if trained* may be somewhat confused at first by the information you send home, and may have numerous questions. They will come to family activities expecting to have changes explained, questions answered, and strategies demonstrated. They may need a personal contact from their child's teacher to follow up the information sent home, and they may have to have a personal invitation from you or their child's teacher before they feel comfortable attending group activities.

Obviously at this point in time each of these three groups has vastly different needs. That is one of the main reasons why keeping the first activity flexible and somewhat unstructured is good planning. Some participants may need only the beginning explanation, after which they can work through the agenda almost on their own. Others will need various degrees of guidance as they work to understand and master the new skills, and you will need to provide for the needs of each of these groups.

PROVIDE MORE DETAILED INFORMATION

After having talked with parents and other community members during your initial information presentation you will have a good idea what their prior knowledge is on the subject of performance-based assessment, and you will probably be able to anticipate in advance what their next questions will be. If a state or local testing initiative has precipitated your efforts to help parents and other community members understand performance-based assessment, there will be specific questions about the new test. The detailed information you give them during Step Two should try to answer those anticipated questions.

The information you provide at this step in the process should be sent home with all students. Your first attempt to provide information to *all* parents and family members comes with a certain amount of risk. You need to remember that not all families will have had the introduction to the ideas that you provided in Step One, so when you send the information home it will be a first exposure for them. You and your teachers should be prepared for some phone calls and notes asking what it is all about and why you are sending it home. Some parents will undoubtedly feel that the information is an imposition, and you should not be surprised to receive complaints. You will have to face the fear and emotions discussed earlier all over again on the part of parents for whom this is the first exposure and who feel uncomfortable with the new ideas.

ESTABLISH A BACKGROUND FOR THE CHANGE

People need to know where new ideas (or old ideas refitted to new purposes) come from. There is a prevailing attitude among the public that educational change is decreed from above and that teachers and students and the needs of society in general have nothing to do with the initiatives. This attitude seems to persist no matter how hard we try to dissuade it, but it is important to try. In the case of performance-based assessment, there are convincing reasons why change is necessary in order to improve education and make high school graduates better prepared for the twenty-first century workplace. This kind of background information needs to be included, although briefly, in any introductory presentation you make. Use it in your introductory remarks, or as background information when you are talking casually with parents and members of your community. A sample introductory speech is included at the end of this chapter (Figure 4.1, p. 63).

Going back to the basic principles mentioned in Chapter 2, there are many examples you can draw from the work world that make intuitive sense to many adults and that help explain clearly why more performance-based strategies are needed in today's schools. Here are some points of interest that have proven to be particularly convincing:

- In the 1950s, 60% of the jobs in this country were unskilled. By the 1990s, unskilled jobs had fallen to less than 20%, with skilled and professional jobs rising to 80%.

- In 1950, 73% of US employees worked in production or manufacturing. Today, that figure has dropped to 15%. In addition, many if not most of the production and manufacturing jobs today involve operating computer-controlled machinery.

- The Department of Labor estimates that in the year 2000, 44% of all workers will be in information-processing jobs. These types of jobs require prior training in the use of computers and other office machinery, which cannot be obtained without meeting specific prerequisites.

- In 1991, for the first time ever, companies spent more money on computing gear than the *combined* monies spent on industrial, mining, farm, and construction equipment.

- It is expected that by the year 2010, all jobs created since the 1990s will require skills that do not exist in the current workforce. This means that a critical skill for the workforce of the future will be the ability to learn new skills and relearn old skills independently.

♦ It used to be that a person could take a machine apart and put it back together and thereby learn how it worked. Many people could be employed simply because of their ability to fix things based on trial and error. Not so today. Mechanics have to use computers to determine what is wrong with car engines.

♦ It used to be that if you had elementary mathematics ability and were willing to risk being the victim of a holdup you could work as a bank teller. Not so today. The banking industry is so complexly automated that some banks have to interview as many as 100 applicants to find *one* potentially trainable teller.

♦ Our work world used to be controlled by management with many people doing tasks that were simple and routine. Not so today. Businesses expect workers to be able to think their way through the workday by analyzing problems, proposing solutions, and effectively managing resources *independently*.

♦ It used to be that even professional jobs were fairly task-specific, with other people to rely on for preliminary or follow-up tasks. Not so today. The best engineers are not worth much if they cannot write their own acceptable project proposals or reports.

Several of these points are presented on sample overheads that you'll find at the end of this chapter (Figures 4.2, p. 65, and 4.3, p. 66).

All of the situations described above relate to skills taught in schools that need to be assessed using performance-based techniques, if schools are going to be certain that students have mastered them.

If you have trouble coming up with examples, call a local business or two and ask the managers or owners to tell you the biggest problems they encounter when trying to find acceptable employees. Use these ideas as you try to establish the background for change in education, and you will find greater understanding among workers in your audience because the examples will be very close to home.

As you present these and other ideas, keep the text short and accompany every idea with a graphic. Graphics serve two purposes when the topic of your presentation is controversial or at the least dubiously viewed. Not only do they help the listener understand the concepts, but they also soften or lighten the impact of the concepts, which, in turn, makes them less threatening.

INTRODUCE SKILLS FOR HELPING AT HOME

Step Two also includes your first organized attempt to introduce parents and other adults to the skills they will need in order to help their children at home with performance-based schoolwork and study.

The first time parents are brought together in a large group to begin learning about performance-based assessment, use a family-style format where the students (who are probably or hopefully already somewhat familiar with the information) attend along with their parents. There is an obvious benefit to this strategy. It helps adults to know that students understand, like, and are competent in the new assessment methods. If parents are basically negative in their attitudes about performance-based assessment, their children's preference for it can disarm the negativity much more quickly than any presentation you can make.

HOW TO DO IT

How to get information out to every parent in your school is always a problem. You want to make sure first of all that it gets to the intended audience. Children are traditionally less than perfect delivery agents! So, you want to make sure that whatever you send is noticeable in the backpack. You also want to make sure the material is pleasing to the eye, easy to understand, informative, and that it provides the information parents need while not overwhelming them. Not a small order! There are many ways to accomplish all of these goals for your informative materials, including but not limited to colorful handouts and news formats. In the case of information about performance-based assessment, however, a more substantial format is probably your best bet. This is especially true if you are trying to inform parents about a specific test administered by your school system or by a state agency.

PARENT HANDBOOK

Handbooks are a staple in the field of education. We seem to have one for everything under the sun. For that reason, parents are accustomed to them and probably keep a collection of them around the house for reference whenever they have a question. That is precisely the reason why you should provide detailed information about your performance-based assessment initiative in the form of a handbook. It is more likely to be retained and used.

According to Barclay and Boone (1996, p. 46), "...handbooks should be neatly presented and easy to read. Wide margins, appealing graphics, and use of varying fonts and type styles serve to make the handbook attractive. Clear headings and subheadings, as well as the inclusion of a table of contents, assist readers in readily locating necessary information. The content should be as brief and direct as possible, yet adequately present the necessary information. And, probably most important, the information should be presented in language that is clear, concise, and free from educational jargon."

Characteristics of Good Handbooks

- ◆ **Wide margins**

- ◆ **Appealing graphics**

- ◆ **Varied fonts and type styles**

- ◆ **Clear headings and subheadings**

- ◆ **Table of Contents**

- ◆ **Brief, direct content**

- ◆ **Clear, concise language**

A list of questions, each answered in a single page, is an effective way to present information. Questions should be arranged in a logical order which anticipates the question readers will have next as they move through the text. Figure 4.4 is one such list.

It can be very challenging to limit the content to answering the question. Remember the joke about the little boy who asked his mother where he came from and she launched into a long discussion about the facts of life? All the child wanted to know was whether he came from Cleveland like his friend Michael! Present enough information to go beyond what you have delivered previously but limit it to what is needed to understand the concepts. Presenting too much information at once can be disastrous, because those who are skeptical or fearful will be *more* so if they do not understand what you are trying to tell them. This is a natural defense mechanism that you want to avoid.

At the end of your handbook, include a list of ideas for what parents can do to help students do well on performance-based assessments and classroom assignments. These suggestions should be brief and easy to implement without additional guidance from school staff. Things such as encouraging children to read for enjoyment, providing tools for mathematics work, and encouraging children to be observant, are general and can be implemented by most parents no matter what their level of understanding of the principles of performance-based assessment. This is a very important element of the information you provide, because many parents, once introduced to the idea that strategies have changed, will be anxious to do things differently right away. You need to give them suggestions that they can implement immediately. Figure 4.5 (p. 54) is a sample list of suggestions for parents.

Figure 4.4: Suggested Series of Questions for Parent Handbook

♦ What is (*the test**)?

♦ Why is (*the test*) important?

♦ How is (*the test*) different from other tests?

♦ What skills do students need?

♦ What subjects are included in (*the test*)?

♦ Who is tested?

♦ Why are (*the tests*) important if my child is not in the (*tested grades*)?

♦ When are students tested?

♦ What are (*the tests*) like?

♦ What does a typical task look like?

♦ How long does it take to complete (*the test*)?

♦ How are students prepared for (*the test*)?

♦ How are (*the tests*) scored?

♦ When do schools find out how students did on (*the tests*)?

♦ What do the scores look like?

♦ What happens if schools do not measure up?

♦ How can I find out what the scores are for my child's school?

♦ How can parents help students do well on (*the test*)?

♦ Where can I get more information?

* Insert the name of your local or state test.

FIGURE 4.5 WHAT PARENTS CAN DO TO HELP

- Encourage your child to read for enjoyment. Talk to your child about what he or she has read. Encourage your child to think hard and to give detailed answers to questions. Help your child compare things that he or she is reading about and relate them to your child's life.

- Help your child learn how to write in complete sentences. Proofread your child's written work and help your child learn to edit his or her own work (to find errors in punctuation, capitalization, and spelling).

- Provide tools for your child to use for mathematics work. A ruler, a compass, a calculator, number cubes, graph paper, and a protractor may be appropriate depending on what grade your child is in. Ask your child's teacher for ideas.

- Help your child learn to be observant, especially in the area of science. Discuss things your child observes and help him or her describe the properties, characteristics, and results of things that happen.

- Help your child learn to summarize in writing things he or she has read or done. Students also need practice putting ideas and definitions into their own words.

- Encourage your child to relate events of the past to current events. Help your child learn to read maps and to give directions.

- Invite your child to go with you to the grocery store. It is a good place to practice math, problem solving, and reading skills.

- Be aware of your child's mental and physical health, especially during testing time. Eating well and getting plenty of rest helps students do their best.

Depending upon your audience, the reading level of your parent handbook may need to be middle school or lower. You may think it a little drastic to use such a low readability level, but keep in mind that you want to reach a very large and diverse population. The students who may have the most difficult time meeting rigorous standards on performance-based tests may also be ones who have parents with limited reading ability. It might be worth a phone call to get information on the literacy level of your population.

For example, the following passages from Calvert County's parent handbook (*The MSPAP: A Handbook for Parents*) that describes a performance-based test have Flesch-Kincaid readability levels of 3.6 (third grade, sixth month) and 4.9 (fourth grade, ninth month) respectively:

What Skills Do Students Need?

Students need to be able to apply what they have learned to real-life problems. To find out if they can do this, schools must give tests that ask students to show what they know and what they can do. These tests are called performance assessments.

How are the Tests Scored?

Teams of teachers work through the summer to read students' answers and assign scores to them. The scores are based on standards that were set up before the test was given. The teachers who score the tests are highly trained and have to pass a test themselves before they can score student responses.

GROUP ACTIVITY

At this point, you are finally ready to invite parents and the community into your school for a *training session*!

We customarily present a program in each school to which parents bring their students to work under the guidance of skilled professionals. The program is specifically designed to *show* the adults what performance-based assessment looks like, why we do it, and what it does to enhance student learning. Four tasks—one each in reading, math, social studies, and science—are used. They are simple and non-threatening. The materials were developed specifically for this purpose, giving the impression of goal-directedness and organization. Skilled professionals are available throughout the activity to answer questions and provide assistance to the parent/child pairs who need it. The success of this step in the overall process revolves, again, around two principles.

First, it is non-threatening. It is nothing like a *workshop* where some adults may feel uncomfortable. It is more like a *family night* where parents and children can be together and share new ideas. We have found that parents do not mind being guided along by their children if that turns out to be the case. To the contrary, they seem to appreciate getting the information from a knowledgeable adult and then having it demonstrated to them by their children.

Secondly, the process serves to codify the methodology. If students have been taking home assignments and other schoolwork that looks different to their parents, the students have most likely been trying to explain the principles and procedures of performance-based assessment to their parents. The parents may not be sure their children are interpreting the ideas correctly, and they (the parents) may hesitate to initiate changes in the way they help their children or guide their homework without being certain they are interpreting the strategies correctly. The family group activity helps parents to see for themselves what it is their children are supposed to be doing, and lets them know whether or not the children have been interpreting the strategies accurately.

Barclay and Boone (1996, p. 103) suggest that although parents want and need strategies to use at home with their children, they also need to understand why the strategies are important and how they will help their child. For this reason it is important that at least a portion of all parent activities be devoted to helping parents understand the rationale behind the practical strategies that will be shared. Understanding why the information is important also increases the chances that parents will actually apply the information at home. Therefore, you should spend a small amount of time at the beginning of this first activity reiterating some of the information presented in the materials previously distributed and going over some very basic theoretical or philosophical points. Keep in mind, however, that most adults will come to this activity ready to see and do, and the faster you move away from the listening part into the seeing and doing part, the happier they will be.

> **To keep children occupied during the introduction, you may want to give them a task to do. One that has been successful for us is having them go to a designated place in the meeting room to pick up the printed materials, pencils, and calculators they will need for the activities. We give the children a list of criteria for completing the task successfully, which includes doing it without talking. They are usually very good about being quiet, because we also tell them that this is their opportunity to show their parents that they can do what they are asked to do. When they return to their seats, they have something to occupy their attention until you are finished with the introduction.**

After the introduction, you will be ready to begin the main activity. Barclay and Boone (1996) recommend the following tips for success:

- ♦ Limit the number of major points to be conveyed;
- ♦ Provide a handout that reinforces them; and
- ♦ Use well-constructed visuals.

Adults and students should work in pairs if possible. Although two adults can work with one child successfully, it is difficult for one adult to work with more than one child. You may want to have *back-up* adults (perhaps teachers, or parents who came without their child). The main objective is for the adults to learn skills for helping children, so it is not essential that they work with their own.

The objectives for the activity should be simple but must facilitate demonstration of the skills you wish the adults to learn. The following objectives are possibilities for this first group meeting:

- ♦ Parents will be able to talk to their children about what they are reading, encourage their children to think hard and to give detailed answers to questions, and to help them compare things that they are reading about and relate them to their own life.

- ♦ Parents will be able to help their children use a calculator for mathematics problem solving.

- ♦ Parents will be able to help their children observe and describe the scientific properties and characteristics of things.

- ♦ Parents will be able to help their children read maps and give directions.

These objectives are direct extensions of the suggestions, found at the end of our parent handbook, for what parents can do to help their children. This provides continuity between one step in our program and the next.

To make suggestions for all of these subject areas in a short amount of time, you may want to carefully select *parts* of typical classroom performance-based tasks rather than use an entire task. We use portions of tasks developed by teachers, portions of tasks from state tests released by the State Department of Education for information purposes, and portions of classroom tasks available to our schools through our membership in the Maryland Assessment Consortium. The tasks used in your first parent activity need to be short and engaging to the students, or they won't willingly serve the purpose of helping their parents learn the assessment process! Each of the ones we use takes about 10 to 20 minutes to complete. They include a reading piece on popular author Chris Van Allsburg, a math activity centered on operating a lemonade stand, a science activity using a magnifying glass to observe four substances that simulate ground covers on a baseball field (puffed rice, rock salt, baby powder, and uncooked long-grain rice), and a map activity.

It is recommended that you avoid using a writing task on the first family group occasion, for two reasons. First, there seems to be greater difference in the ability of adults to accurately guide effective writing than there is to guide other school subjects, and you may not want to inadvertently facilitate ineffective interventions by the adults. Second, when adults work with students on writing samples, especially under the watchful eyes of the children's teachers, they tend to take an unbelievable amount of time doing it!

It is also a good idea to try to select tasks that do not require many or complicated materials. One of the points you will be trying to make is that, although performance-based assessment requires students to demonstrate what they know and can do, it does not require securing or managing a lot of materials. Many classroom tasks utilize common household materials, and you should show adults how using them can be a good way to incorporate performance-based strategies into working with their children at home.

**Household Objects Commonly
Used in Performance Tasks**

- ♦ Cooking utensils such as measuring cups and spoons

- ♦ Tools for linear measure such as rulers, yardsticks and tape measures

- ♦ Substances with texture such as sugar, salt, sand and gravel

- ♦ Small objects that demonstrate floating or sinking

- ♦ Roadmaps, diagrams and pictures

- ♦ Soap, vegetable oil, vinegar, and other non-toxic liquids

- ♦ Wood blocks, tacks, string and rubber bands

- ♦ Dry foods with varied shapes and weights

Explain to the adults that they will be taking the role of the teacher as they work through the tasks with the students. Develop simple instructions for the adults and place them in a separate booklet from the activity pages. Samples for a reading activity (Figure 4.6), a math activity (Figure 4.7, p. 60), a science activity (Figure 4.8, p. 60), and a social studies activity (Figure 4.9, p. 61) can be found on the following pages.

FIGURE 4.6 SAMPLE PARENT GUIDELINES FOR A
READING ACTIVITY—READING AND THINKING TOGETHER

Your child's booklet contains a short story about award-winning author Chris Van Allsburg. Before your child reads the story, ask him or her the following questions to focus his or her attention:

+ What do you think the story is going to be about?

+ Have you ever read anything like this before?

+ Do you remember what happened in what you read before?

+ How do you think this story might be different from the other one?

+ Do you think you are going to like this story?

You can let your child read the story or you can read it out loud yourself. The purpose of this activity is not to see how well your child can read, but how well he or she can think and respond to questions about the story.

After reading the story, ask your child the following questions to help him or her think about what was read. If your child gives one- or two-word answers, encourage him or her to say more.

+ What was the story about?

+ Was it what you expected it to be?

+ Is Chris Van Allsburg a popular author? How do you know?

+ Is writing children's books easy? How do you know?

+ Why does Mr. Van Allsburg leave out details in his drawings?

+ Did the story tell about something you already knew about?

+ What did you learn from the story?

Stop when you have completed this task and wait for further directions.

Figure 4.7 Sample Parent Guidelines for a Mathematics Activity—Using Tools in Mathematics

Your child's booklet contains a math task called *Lemonade Stand* that requires the use of a calculator. Help your child read the task and decide what he or she needs to do first, next, and last. Use these seven steps:

1. Read the entire task.
2. Decide how you will complete the task.
3. Decide what needs to be done first and do it.
4. Decide what needs to be done next and do it.
5. Continue working until the task is finished.
6. Read over the task again.
7. Check your calculations.

Stop when you have completed this task and wait for further directions.

Figure 4.8 Sample Parent Guidelines for a Science Activity—Science Observation

Help your child read and follow the directions for the science task called *Take Me Out to the Ball Field!* Ask your child the following questions after the task is finished.

- ♦ Why were you observing the different substances?
- ♦ Did you know anything about the substances before you started?
- ♦ Did what you already knew help you complete the task?
- ♦ What is the next step in the experiment going to be?
- ♦ What do you think the results will be?

Stop when you have completed this task and wait for further directions.

**FIGURE 4.9 SAMPLE PARENT GUIDELINES FOR
A SOCIAL STUDIES ACTIVITY—MAPS AND DIRECTIONS**

The last task in your child's booklet is a social studies task called *Planning Map for a New Community.* Help your child read and complete the task. After the task is complete, ask your child the following questions:

- How did you know where to find the bridges on the map?

- How could you check to make sure your answer was correct?

- If the compass rose was missing from the map, how would you tell someone how to get from the church to the school?

- Why is knowing how to read a map important?

- Can you think of a time when you have needed a map?

- How do you think real maps are made?

The group leader should briefly explain each activity, tell the adults how much time will be given to complete the task, and ask if anyone has any questions. Assure them that you will let them know when the allotted time is almost up, since task pacing is usually as much of a problem for adults as it is for students, and is a very critical skill during performance assessments. Then the adults should be allowed to work through the activity at an independent pace. The group leader and other professionals should circulate among the participants as they work, encouraging them and answering questions if asked. The professionals also need to watch carefully for groups who finish quickly. Provide discussion and extension of the tasks so that the early completers are not bored while waiting for those working at a more leisurely pace.

At the end of the activity, parents and students should be able to take their materials home so that they will have them to serve as reminders of the skills learned. Ideally, the tasks in this activity should link to future activities, or at least be logical precursors. A small collection of additional tasks would also be a useful take-home handout.

WHEN TO DO IT

We have found that the best time to send home our parent handbook is about two weeks prior to the first family activity. This allows parents to read the detailed information ahead of time and to participate in the family activity while the new ideas are still fresh in their minds.

Some schools prefer to use the handbook and family activity in the late fall, soon after they have given the introductory presentation at their fall open house. Other schools prefer to either split Step Two by using the handbook in the fall and the family activity later in the school year, or by using both in January or March. The schools that wait until March do so because they prefer to provide the detailed information and skills instruction to parents closer to the administration of the state-mandated performance assessment.

When you conduct this step in the process depends largely upon your situation and your goals.

FIGURE 4.1 SAMPLE INTRODUCTORY
SPEECH FOR A PARENT MEETING

It is probably a serious understatement to say that testing has changed significantly over the past 10 to 15 years.

The way we did it in the past was:

♦ We looked at curriculum guides to find out what we were supposed to teach,

♦ We taught,

♦ We made up a test (usually multiple choice, true/false, fill-in-the-blank),

♦ We gave the test to the students, and

♦ We marked down how well they learned the material based on the number of correct answers they got on the test.

This method of testing is good for finding out what students know. However, for many reasons, this method is insufficient for the way education is done today.

For one thing, the sheer volume of information we must teach has mushroomed to the point that we can't possibly teach it all. So instead we have to teach the big ideas, and *also* teach students how to use reasoning skills to find, synthesize, and apply the rest of the available information. The trouble is, our traditional method of testing (selected response) cannot efficiently tell us whether or not students can find, synthesize, and apply. These are not things that we can just *know*—they are things we must be *able to do*.

Secondly, schooling today involves many more of what we call *skills*—things we expect students to be *able to do*. The number of skills needed just to exist in a modern world has also mushroomed. It is one thing to be able to turn a switch on and off (which is what I needed to be able to do with the two appliances I had in my kitchen when I was married) and quite another thing to be able to program four different appliances with computers in them (which is what I need to be able to do with the numerous appliances I have in my kitchen now). Traditional methods of testing cannot adequately determine whether or not I am able to program those appliances. In order for someone who is teaching me to say for sure that I know how to do it, I have to *demonstrate* my ability.

Thirdly, selected response testing has too much room for mismeasurement—which means making us think the students know things when they are actually just guessing. A 20 to 25% chance that the student is getting the answer correct just by guessing is not a satisfactory error of measurement in the twenty-first century. Society, especially the business world, is no longer satisfied to accept that high level of mismeasurement.

So testing has taken on a dimension that was not needed as much in the past. Testing today must not only determine what students *know,* but also what they *can do.* We call this kind of testing *performance assessment.*

Methods of developing tests have had to change along with the formats. Knowing *what* to teach is not enough. We simply cannot develop efficient, equitable tests without agreeing ahead of time on exactly what it is we expect students to know and be able to do. We also have to know when they need to know it (by the end of first grade, or third grade, or seventh grade, etc.), and how well they need to know it. All of these things determine *how* we teach.

All of this has led to the need for educators to develop a new way of specifying what it is we expect students to know and be able to do. We now develop documents called *standards.* There are standards developed by many professional organizations (such as the National Council of Teachers of Mathematics), standards developed by individual states, standards developed by the US government, standards developed by school systems, and standards developed by individual schools. These documents tell us what is expected of students and therefore what should be on our tests.

The next step is to develop tests that consistently and fairly assess how well we are all achieving what it is we intend. The tests are developed using the standards documents as a basis. The documents tell us whether students need to know something or if they need to be able to do something. And if they need to be able to do something, they tell us how—-list, describe, compare, analyze, find, outline, search and select, self-correct, predict, relate, summarize, locate, gather, build, connect, measure, communicate, etc. The documents are essentially guides for teaching and testing.

The tests that are developed from these documents must allow students to show what they know. They look different from traditional tests, they are administered differently, they sometimes take longer, and they provide us with much more detailed information about students' abilities. Tonight we will be showing you what performance assessment looks like and how it is accomplished. You will have an opportunity to work through some sample tasks with your child. We hope that you will find this information and experience useful, especially in terms of how you help your children study and prepare for tests in their classrooms."

Figure 4.2 Sample Overhead 1—
Skilled vs. Unskilled Jobs

In the 1950s, 60% of the jobs in this country were unskilled. By the 1990s, unskilled jobs had fallen to less than 20%, with skilled and professional jobs rising to 80%.

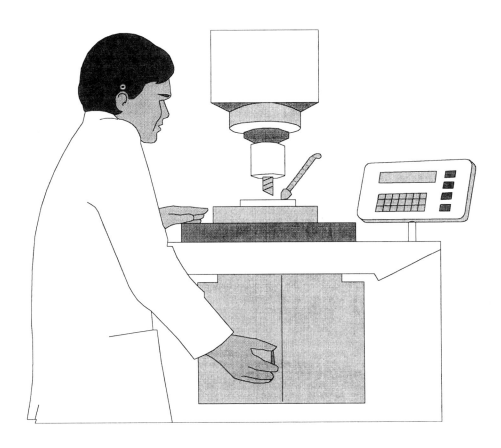

**FIGURE 4.3 SAMPLE OVERHEAD 2—
MECHANICS AND COMPUTERS**

Today, mechanics have to use computers to determine what is wrong with car engines.

5

STEP THREE: TEACHING PERFORMANCE-BASED SKILLS TO PARENTS

According to researcher Joyce Epstein (1986) 85% of parents, regardless of socioeconomic background, spend time helping their children at home when asked to do so by the teacher (an important qualifier). And they would spend more time helping their children at home if they had more guidance about what they should do. In spite of being willing and wanting to know how, though, few show up when we offer opportunities to come in to the school to learn the necessary skills. Educators expend a lot of time and energy trying to find successful lures! In spite of our efforts, the majority of parents do not take advantage of the opportunities we provide, and we have to face this outcome head-on when new initiatives make it imperative that we reeducate our parent population. We have to find ways to get parents to come, and then we have to give them exactly what they want and need once they get there. This is an awesome task!

WHAT TO DO

It is only during the third step in the process of helping parents and the community to understand performance-based assessment that you should invite parents to a workshop format where they have intensive involvement in the fundamentals of performance-based assessment. The difference between Step Two and Step Three is the intensity of the content. At the third step, you should provide direct and detailed information about the topic and guide parents through more complex examples of the methodology. You may also demonstrate more involved links between instruction and assessment. More detailed documentation in the form of handouts may be used, and more specific suggestions for helping students complete assignments and study in general may be included.

PARENT ROLES AS INSTRUCTORS

Those who are *experts* may be well beyond the need for assistance with helping their children. They may be at the point of intuitive understanding whenever something new or different shows up in homework or on assessments. Don't be disappointed if they decline your invitation to training activities. Those who do attend, however, will expect to be shown succinctly what to do and how to do it, and may not need much practice. Don't be insulted if they get what they need from the presentation (or from the handouts) and then quietly slip out.

Parents who are *competent* will expect to be shown thoroughly what to do and how to do it, and will need some practice. Their expectations will be clear and it would be a good idea to ask about those expectations at the beginning of the activity. There may be a wide range of readiness for new skills among this group of parents at this time, and you should try your best to uncover the degrees of readiness and to provide for the needs of each person.

Those who are *skilled if trained* will expect to be shown patiently what to do and how to do it, and will require extended practice. As skills become more complex, you will need to break them down into manageable parts and to do so without seeming to *water down* the concepts to a level that might seem insulting to some persons. It is at this point that there is danger you will *lose* some of them if they do not go away feeling comfortable with the skills you are teaching them.

PROVIDE GUIDED INSTRUCTION

Much education takes place on a moment-to-moment basis (Delgado-Gaitan, 1990, p. 47), therefore it is important to help parents learn how to make the strategies of performance-based assessment part of their everyday lives. Some things need to become second nature. Unfortunately, most skills cannot become second nature without a lot of practice. Your workshops for parents on performance-based assessment should focus on a few universal skills that you can demonstrate quickly. Then you should devote the majority of the workshop time to providing guided practice, with the goal of having participants close to mastery by the end of the workshop. It is best to begin with a few strategies that seem most important, and then to expand the repertoire as the parents are able to handle more.

HOW TO DO IT

Can you think of an educator who approaches the prospect of doing a workshop for parents with unlimited eagerness and positive anticipation? If you can, that educator has probably never before tried to do it. This is not to say that workshops are *never* successful, but they *are* frequently difficult to plan, difficult to staff, and difficult to tailor to the specific needs of the audience. Recruitment is often less than successful from the educator's point of view. So why is the next recommended step in the process of helping parents and the community understand performance-based assessment organizing and holding a workshop? Because this is the point at which you need to provide the opportunity for parents to receive extended, face-to-face instruction, and workshops are the only way to effectively do this.

WORKSHOPS

The best way to teach parents how to help their children at home is to model the skills you want them to learn. In the case of performance-based assessment, the best way to do this is to set up an authentic performance task, demonstrate how the teacher presents the task and interacts with the students during the task, and let parents have the opportunity to imitate what the teacher does. Figures 5.1 (p. 73), 5.2 (p. 80), and 5.3 (p. 84), at the end of this chapter, are sample tasks that are usable for this purpose.

> **The best way to teach parents how to help their children at home is to model the skills you want them to learn.**

Probably the most important skill parents need to have is the ability to guide students through homework and other learning activities without doing the work for them. Performance-based assessment and instruction require students to work independently. Students must know how to interpret text into required steps in a process, when to refer back to the text, what to do first, next, and last, and how to judge when a task is completed to the level of expectation of the teacher or assessor. Many students (whether gifted, average, or at-risk) do not perform as well as they could because of their inability to do these things. For one reason or another, they are accustomed to a lot of prompting and monitoring. The world of work requires adults to work without prompting and monitoring, and therefore students in school need to be taught these skills.

Parents need to know how to guide this process. Among other things, they need to know how much information to give without damaging the validity of the task as an assessment tool. They need to know what questions to ask that stimulate thinking without giving away the answer to the task. They need to know techniques for helping students pace themselves through tasks in order to finish within time limits. And they need to know how to guide students through an evaluation of their work to determine if it meets the standards expected for quality performance.

Guiding the Performance-Based Assessment Process

♦ **How much information should I give?**

♦ **What questions should I ask to stimulate thinking?**

♦ **What are some techniques for pacing student work?**

♦ **How do we know if the work meets the standards?**

Another skill that is good as a beginning is *reflective reading*. Reflective reading helps the reader better understand the material because it creates links between prior knowledge and new information, helps link individual concepts as we read them, and helps us pose questions which need clarification. As adults we constantly think as we read, but of course, we do not usually voice our thoughts aloud. Modeling this process is the best way to teach children how to do it. When adults consciously utilize this skill when reading to and with children, the children not only learn the skill itself but also have the benefit of the adult's interpretation and understanding of the text.

If you are using graphic organizers, charts, and procedural activities in the classroom, now is the time to share them with parents. Not only will they be able to extend the utilization of the devices to the home, but the devices themselves can also be educational. An example is a set of posters we use to help students respond effectively on reading tests. We teach the students that there are three different purposes for reading (to be informed, for literary experience, and to perform a task), and we teach them that there are four different ways in which they might be asked to respond to the text (global understanding, developing interpretation, personal reflection, and critical stance/author's craft). We have charts posted in every classroom, and students regularly refer to the charts as they respond to assignments and assessments. We produce duplicates of the posters for individual student use, and encourage students to use them until they are so familiar with the techniques that they do not need any assistance. If we send the poster replicas home without any explanation or training for parents, their usefulness is almost negative. But if parents know the principles behind the practice and know how to guide students in using the charts, their usefulness is greatly enhanced.

The content of your workshops will depend on the nature of your assessments. You may want to start with some general skills like the ones outlined above. Or you might want to start with specific skills that relate to your standards or learning objectives. If your assessments are made up of combined assessment methods, you should help parents understand the differences between types of test items and add discriminated response techniques to the list of skills they need to learn. No matter what you choose in the way of content, the key to success at this step in the overall process is to keep the content as simple as possible and to make sure the participants have enough time to practice. Because it is so difficult to get parents to come to school for workshops, we have a tendency to try to cram a lot of skills and techniques into one workshop. You are better off avoiding this tendency and making sure your workshops (especially the first one) are not overwhelming, so that parents will come back for another one. Remember the fear and anxiety issues discussed in Chapter 1!

Many schools implement this step in the same manner in which the second step is done, that is with parents and students working together. Other schools work with parents alone. Sometimes a conference or menu program is used. Although we prefer the family-style format, your participant group may prefer workshops for adults only. If that is the case, you will have to adapt your example tasks to adults rather than children, and your presentation will probably include some role-playing or group work to give the parents the opportunity to practice.

Parent workshops need to be informal in order to foster a friendly and supportive atmosphere (Jones, 1991, p. 30), and there are many ways to do this. The location of the activity might be a classroom or library instead of a large space such as the cafeteria. You might provide snacks and beverages, or, as is the case with one of the sample tasks at the end of this chapter, the tasks might revolve around a family activity such as an ice cream sundae party. If childcare is available, parents will be more likely to be able to attend. Presenters could wear comfortable clothes and shoes instead of business attire. If parents feel comfortable and perceive the environment to be friendly and supportive, they will come away with a more positive attitude about the topic which, as discussed earlier, is an important aspect of your efforts to educate them about performance-based assessment.

Although delivery method is always an important factor in the success of parent workshops, it is really important in instances where they are insecure about the topic and somewhat dubious about the value of the practices they are being taught. To reduce the possibility that some participants may feel a little threatened by the content or the workshop situation, some schools use volunteer parents as group leaders for workshops. This requires an additional step in the process, because your group leaders have to be trained. But it is worth considering depending upon the level of anxiety among the participants.

Characteristics of Effective Workshops

- ◆ **Leaders act as models, not lecturers.**

- ◆ **Concise, useful handouts are provided.**

- ◆ **Content goes from general to specific.**

- ◆ **An informal setting is used.**

- ◆ **A friendly and supportive atmosphere is maintained.**

- ◆ **A familiar location is used.**

- ◆ **Group leaders are non-threatening.**

Location is another element that can have an important impact on attendance. Some schools have found that going to parents and the community in places where they have already congregated is more successful than asking parents to come to the school. There are numerous places in every community where this might be possible. It might be worth your while to explore some of these possibilities.

Family learning centers are another way of offering assistance to parents. This approach allows them to explore new ideas on their own terms. If you can design your workshops so that they can be used by parents on an individual, self-paced basis, you will greatly increase their usefulness. Multiple levels of interaction and information can be provided to cover the needs of various individuals, and children can be included without the need to plan numerous activities for several grade and ability levels.

WHEN TO DO IT

Workshops should follow your other activities at a sensible interval, with consideration for the informational needs of the target audience. Some parents may feel more comfortable with a little bit of time between activities so that they are able to absorb information at their own rate. Others may make it clear that they need the next step in the process soon after the previous one. You may find that when you get to the workshop stage you need to have them on more than one occasion and at more than one time of the day. Keep in mind that, depending upon the needs of your parents as you move through the process, the impact on your students' performance may be limited unless you conduct the activities well in advance of the assessments.

FIGURE 5.1 FAMILY NIGHT ACTIVITIES—
ICE CREAM SUNDAES

TEACHER DIRECTIONS

Ice cream is one of America's favorite desserts. This evening you will be making your own ice cream sundae. You and your family will be completing several activities about ice cream.

Activity 1 (Reading)

First you will be reading to perform a task. When you read to perform a task, you may want to use the following strategies.

♦ When reading directions, think about:

- What the directions are asking the reader to do

- How the author organized the directions to help the reader

♦ Before reading:

- Look over and preview the material.

♦ During reading:

- Read the material once and then read it again.

- Circle the *do* words.

- Use illustrations, pictures, or labeled diagrams the author has provided for you.

- Pause after each direction you read and make a mind picture of what you are being asked to do.

♦ After reading:

- Decide if you would be able to perform the task easily as written.

- Do the directions include all of the items that make it a well written set of directions? (Title, materials list, numbered steps, illustrations or labeled diagrams, easy-to-read headings)

- Do you need to go back and reread the text to make sure you understand?

You will have 10 minutes to read and complete Activity 1.

Activity 2 (Mathematics)

You will have 10 minutes to read and complete Activity 2.

Activity 3 (Mathematics)

You will have 10 minutes to read and complete Activity 3.

Activity 4 (Writing/Language Usage)

You will have 15 minutes to complete Activity 4.

STUDENT PAGES

Activity 1

Your class is planning a spring party. Everyone wants to make it a *Build-Your-Own Ice Cream Sundae* party. Your teacher has agreed but needs help in planning it. The class is considering making their own ice cream for the party. Two students have brought in recipes to be considered.

Ice Cream Recipe

In a large zip-lock bag place 4-5 cubes of ice. Add 2 tablespoons of salt to the ice. In a smaller zip-lock bag, place ½ cup of milk, ¼ teaspoon of vanilla, and 4 teaspoons of sugar. For chocolate ice cream, use chocolate milk. Seal the smaller bag and place it within the larger bag. Seal the larger bag. Shake the larger bag for approximately 5 minutes. Remove the smaller bag, open, and *enjoy*!

Chocolatey Ice Cream

What you will need:	1 large coffee can with lid	2 tablespoons salt
	1 small coffee can with lid	½ cup chocolate milk
	tray of ice cubes (crushed)	¼ teaspoon vanilla
		4 teaspoons sugar

How to Make Your Ice Cream

- ◆ First, put the ice in the large coffee can.
- ◆ Then add 2 tablespoons of salt to the ice in the large can.
- ◆ Next, in the small can, add the milk, vanilla, and sugar. Seal the can.
- ◆ Now, place the smaller can *inside* the larger can. Seal the larger can.
- ◆ Shake or roll the larger can for about 5 or 10 minutes.
- ◆ Remove the smaller can.
- ◆ Open the can and serve!

Task 1

Which recipe would be easier to make? Use information from both recipes to support your choice.

_____

_____

_____

_____

Task 2

What would you add, take away, or change to make the first recipe easier to follow?

_____

_____

_____

_____

Stop and wait for further directions.

Activity 2

After reviewing the recipes, the class has decided to purchase the ice cream needed for the party. The class must decide how much ice cream will be needed. 25 students, 1 teacher, and 1 principal will be attending the party. Each person will use approximately 2 cups of ice cream. Your teacher wants to buy the large gallon-size containers of ice cream. Each gallon contains 16 cups of ice cream.

Task 1

Using the information above, calculate how many gallons of ice cream will be needed for the party. _____

Task 2

The cafeteria manager will purchase the ice cream. A gallon of ice cream costs $4.50. How much money will the manager need to purchase enough ice cream for the party? _____

Task 3

The principal will donate all of the toppings for the sundaes but the students will each have to contribute some money towards the cost of the ice cream. Explain how you could find the amount of money each student should contribute.

_____

_____

_____

_____

Stop and wait for further directions.

Activity 3

Your class must now decide which flavor of ice cream to order for the party. Your teacher has decided to survey the class. On the chart below you will find the results of the class survey.

FLAVOR	TALLY MARKS
Chocolate	/ / / / / /
Vanilla	/ / /
Strawberry	/ / / / / / /
Chocolate Chip	/ / / /
Cookies and Cream	/ / / / /

Task 1

Using the data on the chart, complete the bar graph showing the results.

Title: Class Survey on Favorite Ice Cream Flavors

Chocolate   Vanilla   Strawberry   Chocolate Chip   Cookies & Cream

Task 2

What was the most popular flavor? _____
Explain your answer.

_____

_____

_____

_____

Stop and wait for further directions.

Activity 4

You have just completed a survey about favorite ice cream flavors. The cafeteria manager is going to buy the ice cream for your party. She believes that cookies and cream is the best flavor. Write a letter to persuade her to buy the most popular flavor from the survey.

When you write to persuade, you want to convince someone else to do or think about something the way you do. When you write to persuade, you want to do the following:

♦ Decide what your position or stand is on the topic.

♦ Think of your reasons for that position or stand.

♦ Organize the reasons for your position.

♦ Invite/convince your reader to share your position.

Before you begin, think about:

♦ F   What is the form of your writing? _____

♦ A   Who is your audience? _____

- ◆ T   What is the topic? _____
- ◆ P   What is the purpose? _____
- ◆ IG   What information should be included?

_____

_____

_____

_____

Now, write your letter below.

April 1, 2000

Dear _____,

_____

_____

_____

_____

_____

_____

_____

_____

_____

_____

_____

_____

_____

_____

_____

_____

_____

_____

**FIGURE 5.2 FAMILY NIGHT ACTIVITIES—
REUADING**

STUDENT PAGES

Reading to be Informed

Today you will read to be informed. When you read to be informed, you may want to use the following strategies.

Think About:

- The topic/main idea of the selection;

- What information you may already know about the topic/main idea;

- What you may want to know/learn about the topic in this selection.

Before Reading

- Look over what you will read.

- Skim/preview to find out how the author has chosen to present the material.

- Ask a question about the topic that you hope to find out.

During Reading

- Read the material carefully (slowly).

- Pay attention to chapters, titles, illustrations, bold type print and captions.

- Pause during your reading to organize new information and to link it to what you already know.

After Reading

- Think about something you may not have understood. *Go back* and reread that part.

- Use resources, such as the dictionary, when you are unable to make sense of the selection.

- Go back and think about your original question. Can you answer it?

- Think about what you have learned as a result of reading. How does it compare to what you already knew about the topic?

You will have 30 minutes to complete this task. Now read "1999 Brings 24 New Beanie Babies" and complete Activities 1 to 4.

1999 Brings 24 New Beanie Babies

On January 1, 1999, Ty, the maker of Beanie Babies, announced that they would be releasing 24 new Beanies. The Ty Company thought hard about the design of these new Beanies. They wanted to release Beanies that were different from any they had ever made before. The 24 new Beanies they chose to release have caused Beanie collectors of all ages to go wild.

The most popular type of Beanie to collect is the *sit-up* bear. The Erin and Princess bears are examples of this type. In the January 1999 release there were six of this style bear. It has been reported that these new bears are selling for $100.00 each.

Kicks has been the most popular of the new bears. It is light green with a soccer ball on its chest. This bear is not only popular with Beanie collectors, but also with soccer moms and soccer players. Many people predict that this is just the first of many *sport* bears that Ty will release.

The *1999 Signature* bear is also very popular among collectors. Since this bear is dated, it is almost certain to be retired at the end of the year. This bear is brown with a red heart on its chest. On the heart is an embroidered "TY," which is the signature of the company.

Valentina is being released to replace the retired *Valentino*. She is dark pink in color and has a white heart on her chest.

Many say that the new bear named *Fuzz* is exactly like the retired bear *Curly*. Fuzz and Curly are both made from brown furry fabric. The only real difference is that Curly has a dark red ribbon around his neck and Fuzz has a blue one.

The *Millennium* bear is a purple bear with a millennium symbol sewn on its chest. This bear was released in honor of the year 2000. Collectors are hoping it will be valuable since "millennium" is spelled incorrectly on the tag.

Along with these five bears, Ty also released three other bears. *Hope* is a tan bear that kneels as though it is praying. *Germania* is another sit up bear, but will only be released in Germany. The last of the bears is *Sammy the Cub*. He is a tie-dyed bear that is lying down. Sammy is in honor of Sammy Sosa, the Chicago Cub who tried to break the home run record last year. Ty also released a red cardinal, *Mac*, in honor of St. Louis Cardinal, Mark Maguire, who broke the record for most home runs in a season.

Although these new bears are the most popular among the collectors, the other 15 releases are just as great and hard to find. The collection includes a stork, seal, three dogs, three rabbits, a lamb, a chick hatching from an egg, a jellyfish, a hedge hog, a kitten, a mountain goat, and a spider monkey. We wonder what Ty will think of next!

Now, complete the following activities.

Activity 1 (Global Understanding)

What information about Beanie Babies could someone learn by reading this article?

_____

_____

_____

_____

Activity 2 (Critical Stance)

List three things that the author needed to know before she could write this article.

A. _____

B. _____

C. _____

Activity 3 (Critical Stance)

Do you think the author did a good job informing us about the new Beanie Babies? Use support from the text in your answer.

_____

_____

_____

_____

Activity 4 (Writing Connection)

The Ty Company is asking kids for their help in designing the next Beanie bear. They want the bear to be a sport bear.

Think about a design for a new Beanie Baby. It must be a design that is related to a sport. You may want to make a brief sketch of your design.

Then, write a letter persuading the company to choose your design. You may want to use a graphic organizer to plan your letter before you begin writing. Use the space below for your sketch and graphic organizer. Then write your letter in the additional space provided.

Dear Ty Company:

_____

_____

_____

_____

_____

_____

_____

_____

_____

_____

_____

_____

_____

_____

_____

_____

Sincerely,

FIGURE 5.3 FAMILY NIGHT ACTIVITIES— TEXT OF PARENT HANDOUT PAMPHLET

STRATEGIC READERS BLAST INTO READING

Reading for Literary Experience
Before Reading

- Look at the title and illustrations to help you make predictions.

- Choose 1 or 2 purposes for reading the selection.

During Reading

- Look for descriptive words or phrases that help to make the characters come alive.

- Stop and retell the important events.

- Think about what might happen next as you read the story.

After Reading a Play or Story, Think About

- Your purposes for reading the selection.

- How the author made the text seem real or make-believe.

- The setting.

- The physical traits and the character traits (personality) of the main characters.

- The problems/solutions or the goals of the main characters.

- A summary of the plot.

- How you would have reacted if you were one of the characters.

Reading to Perform a Task
Before Reading

- Look at the illustrations, bold-face print, diagrams, or charts.

- Read the directions.

During Reading

♦ Carefully read the directions once and then read them again.

♦ Stop after each direction. Make a picture in your mind of what you are asked to do.

♦ Study the illustrations, bold-face print, diagrams, or charts.

♦ Think about problems you might have in performing the task.

After Reading

♦ Decide if the directions are organized in a way that would be easy for you to follow.

♦ If the directions or steps are not numbered, use your pencil to number the steps in sequential order.

♦ Gather together all the needed materials and complete the task.

Reading to be Informed

Before Reading

♦ Look over the material that you will read.

♦ Decide what you want to learn or find out.

During Reading

♦ Study titles, illustrations, charts, captions, and bold-face print.

♦ Change subtitles into questions as you read.

♦ Underline or highlight important information.

♦ Reread parts that are confusing or unclear.

After Reading

♦ Think about what you have learned.

♦ Reread the information that you highlighted or underlined.

♦ Think about what you still want to learn.

Strike it Rich with Testing Tips

Before the Test

- ◆ Get a good night's rest.

- ◆ Eat a good breakfast.

- ◆ Dress comfortably.

- ◆ Determine to do your very best.

- ◆ Have an "I can do it" attitude.

During the Test

- ◆ Listen carefully to all directions.

- ◆ Reread directions as much as you need to (at least twice).

- ◆ Highlight and number all the *do* words.

- ◆ Use you highlighter to highlight important information.

- ◆ Answer all the parts of the question.

- ◆ Use your resources—dictionary, thesaurus, etc.

- ◆ Pay attention to the writing icons.

- ◆ Reread your answers. Revise them if you need to.

- ◆ Pace yourself. Be aware of how much time you have left.

After the Test

- ◆ Celebrate your successes!

- ◆ Congratulate yourself on a job well done.

- ◆ Reflect on what you learned.

- ◆ Think about what you can do to do better next time.

6

STEP FOUR: HELPING PARENTS PRACTICE PERFORMANCE-BASED SKILLS

The last step in the process of helping parents and the community understand performance-based assessment is the most critical to the endurance of your efforts. Once parents have learned new strategies, they must be able to maintain them. The strategies they learned as students themselves have been part of them for so long that the new strategies will slip out of habit unless they are continually renewed and reinforced. For that reason, you aren't ever finished being involved with helping them understand performance-based assessment!

WHAT TO DO

After introducing the concept, sharing knowledge about it, and teaching parents about performance-based assessment, you will need to provide opportunities for parents to practice the strategies at home on a continuing basis. The most effective way to do this is by having classroom teachers provide frequent opportunities for parents to implement strategies at home that reinforce the processes and procedures students are learning in school.

An important aspect of this step is that strategies should be personalized for the parents as well as for their children. According to Kahn (1996, p. 58), schools have been criticized over the years because parents perceive the efforts of schools to involve them as merely ritualistic. Parents sometimes feel that schools invite them to be involved because it is the thing to do or because it is expected, then fail to follow through with relevant, meaningful suggestions for things parents can do to help their children succeed. To avoid this perception, this final step in the process of helping parents and the community understand performance-based assessment must be individually relevant to what students are learning in school and must clearly demonstrate that there is an important link between what happens in school and what parents are doing at home to help their children learn.

There is a significant caution that has to be raised here. Up to this point, your efforts have been voluntarily received by those who want to participate, or (in the case of the handbook and other materials sent home to all students) freely ignored by those who do not support your initiative or are, for one reason or another, simply not interested. Sending activities home for parents and students to work on together, however, may involve assigned work that contributes to students' grades.

You need to take into consideration the fact that many parents will not have attended previous activities, will not be prepared to help their children, and some may even resent what they consider to be an imposition when you imply that they should do so. Your staff needs to decide in advance how they will collectively cope with these possibilities and have a plan of approach in mind. If parents cannot or will not provide assistance at home, will you provide assistance for students in class? Will you provide adult or older student mentors for them? Will the assignments be graded, or will they be totally voluntary? The answers to these and other questions that come up as a result of parent attitudes and readiness to help will depend upon many things, not the least of which is the make-up of your population and their specific needs. If you believe you have reached only a small proportion of your parent population with prior activities, you must approach this final step with that in mind.

PARENT ROLES AS INSTRUCTORS

Parents who can be characterized as experts will appreciate periodic updated information because it will allow them to tailor their assistance to the curriculum and the skills currently being emphasized in class. They will read materials sent home selectively, picking out what they can use and even adapting it to their child's specific needs. They will be an excellent source of feedback, and may even be a source of ideas for follow-up or extension tasks. You should invite them to freely respond to the materials you send home and to help in the design of activities.

Parents who can be characterized as competent instructors will expect periodic updated information because they will rely on their child's teacher to show them what needs to be done next. They will read materials sent home carefully and will probably not hesitate to call the teacher if they have a question. They, also, will be a good source of feedback and will provide you with good ideas about how to revise activities to make them more easily understood and implemented.

Parents who can be characterized as skilled if trained will require periodic updated information in order to know what to do next and in order to have their new skills reinforced regularly. They will read materials carefully and may have questions. It might be worthwhile for teachers to contact these parents by telephone or by note after the first few activities are sent home. The contacts will serve two purposes. First, parents in this group are less likely to initiate contact with the teacher, especially if they do not understand what they are expected to do, and so the teacher needs to take the initiative. Second, it is a good idea to clarify the purpose and procedures of the activity even if it seems like there will be no questions. By clarifying, the teacher has the opportunity to reinforce and extend the parents' own learning and strengthen the parents' skills.

PROVIDE FREQUENT, RELEVANT OPPORTUNITIES TO PRACTICE

Frequent, relevant opportunities to practice can be provided through interactive homework assignments designed to guide parents through the helping skills previously learned, while at the same time reinforcing concepts and skills students have learned in class.

"Helping with homework has traditionally been the major form of interface between parents, their children, and the school" (Jones, 1991, p. 28). Schools expect parents to create an environment at home that encourages students to do their homework, and are frequently called upon to interpret assignments, re-teach concepts, guide their children through the steps in the practice process, and to review completed homework for correctness. This expectation stems from numerous studies over the years that have shown that the way in which parents "organize natural learning environments in the home as part of their everyday lives…" can influence student achievement (Delgado-Gaitan, 1990, p. 45).

Unfortunately, interpreting assignments, re-teaching concepts, guiding children through the steps in the practice process, and reviewing completed homework for correctness are not always accomplished in the same way for performance-based assignments as they are for more traditional types of assignments. Homework assignments that are intended to help parents maintain the skills you have taught them should focus on these four known facilitating skills as well as on the specific skills introduced in your workshops.

An interactive homework process similar to the one developed by researchers at Johns Hopkins University and teachers in Maryland, Virginia, and the District of Columbia may be an excellent way to help parents practice their new skills. Called TIPS (Teachers Involve Parents in Schoolwork), the Johns Hopkins program involves a sequence of homework assignments that require parent interaction. Parents monitor, interact, and support their children, but they are not asked to teach school subjects or to read or direct the assignments that are the students' responsibilities (Epstein, Simon, & Salinas, 1997). Each assignment includes a section for home-to-school communication in which parents indicate whether the student was able to discuss the homework, whether they enjoyed working on the activity together, and whether they learned something about what the student is learning in class. Through these assignments, students are able to show parents exactly how they learned a skill in class and parents gain information about the school curriculum and their children's work. Activities require only inexpensive or no-cost materials that are readily available at home.

How to Do It

Teachers should provide frequent homework assignments that guide parents through such skills as:

- Helping students interpret text into required steps in a process;
- Helping students know when and how to refer back to the text when seeking support for a response;
- Helping students learn to sequence and pace tasks;
- Helping students find information from supplemental sources;
- Asking stimulus questions; and
- Helping students use graphic organizers.

Teacher-Developed Activities

A series of articles with reproducible worksheets written by Joyce Epstein appeared in *Instructor* magazine between September 1993 and May/June 1994. If you can find them, the worksheets may serve as good examples of the kinds of assignments teachers can send home to help parents maintain their skills as they also help their children complete performance-based assignments. There are also two examples developed by the author at the end of this chapter (Figures 6.1, p. 92, and 6.2, p. 93). Notice that in addition to supporting the skills the students have been learning in class (geometric shapes and patterns), the first one is specifically designed to help parents guide students through sequencing a task in an efficient manner.

There are several things teachers can do to make interactive homework assignments more easily understood and easier to implement at home. In terms of format, these include keeping the assignment to a single page, using plenty of white space to segment sub-steps in the task, using borders and varied fonts to accentuate important information or directions, giving space to respond whenever possible (the amount of space provided is a clue to parents about how much students are expected to write), and being consistent from activity to activity in format and style.

WHEN TO DO IT

Interactive homework assignments are more successful when they take little time and when parents and students have several days to complete them. If you expect parents to work with their children, you have to keep in mind that many parents work and have obligations outside the home. They may be overburdened by an assignment that is expected back the next day, and if they are not enthusiastic about completing it, you will not achieve your desired effect.

Interactive assignments may best be sent home on Wednesdays or Thursdays with the expectation that they be returned on the following Monday. This allows families who have weekend plans to get them done before the weekend, and also allows those who are too tired or busy to do them during the week to wait until the weekend.

Setting up a schedule for interactive homework activities may be a good idea. Teachers may agree to send them home once a week, every other week, or once a month on the first Friday. Alternatively, they might be sent home at the end of every unit or chapter, following every chapter or unit test, just prior to every test, or at any other interval that seems to be practical and acceptable to parents and teachers alike. If parents know when to expect the activities, they can budget their time and be prepared to complete them with little stress.

Regardless of when the activities are sent home, the most important factor in their success is regularity and persistence. Your efforts to help parents understand performance-based assessment will be most effective if you continue to provide frequent and relevant opportunities to practice the skills you want them to use at home for as long as you are using performance-based assessment and learning in your school.

FIGURE 6.1 HOME/SCHOOL PERFORMANCE TASK—
GEOMETRIC SHAPES

We have been studying geometric shapes and patterns. This task will give students a chance to apply what they have learned to a situation that might actually happen in the real world.

Materials Needed: paper, pencil, crayons or colored pencils, scissors, tape

Assignment:

Suppose that a jewelry store at the mall is having its 25-year anniversary and wants to have a special ring to sell during the celebration. The store designer has decided to have a contest for the design of the ring. The gem cutter has said that the ring can have stones of any shape, but they must be arranged in a symmetrical pattern. The winning design will receive a prize of $100. Pretend you have decided to enter the contest. Use the strip below to design your pattern. Then cut out the strip and tape the ends together to make a ring.

Decide which shapes you want to use in your design and write them here.

_____

Decide what color each shape will be. Draw and color the shapes here.

Decide how you will arrange the shapes in a repeated pattern and sketch it.

Describe your pattern in writing.

_____

_____

_____

Now, draw and color your pattern in the strip. Then make your strip symmetrical. After you have finished, cut out the strip and tape the ends together to make a ring.

FIGURE 6.2 HOME/SCHOOL PERFORMANCE TASK—
ADDITION AND SUBTRACTION

This task gives students a chance to apply addition and subtraction skills to a situation that might actually happen in the real world.

Materials Needed: paper, pencil, calculator

Assignment:

Suppose that your aunt recently started a new job as a pilot for a small local airline. She will receive a bonus when she has flown 10,000 miles. She has already flown 4,800 miles and wants to get her bonus before the winter holidays, which are just 2 weeks away. She has promised you that if she reaches her goal, she will take you to Disney World over the holidays. She is allowed to work four days per week and fly one round-trip each day. She cannot go to the same city two days in a row. Using the mileage table below, decide where she will need to go in order to reach her goal.

How many more miles does your aunt have to fly to get her bonus? _____

Explain how you got your answer.

_____

_____

Use the table to make up a daily schedule that will allow your aunt to meet her goal. List the cities and the number of miles for each *round trip* on the lines below.

	City	Miles
Day 1	_____ /	_____
Day 2	_____ /	_____
Day 3	_____ /	_____
Day 4	_____ /	_____
Day 5	_____ /	_____
Day 6	_____ /	_____
Day 7	_____ /	_____
Day 8	_____ /	_____

Flying Distance to Cities Served by YourTown Airline

City	Miles One Way
Desert Gulch	322
Big Rapids	340
Paradise	245
Canyon Alley	363

On the back of the paper, answer these questions:

1. How did you know which cities to choose?

2. Is there any other way you could arrange your aunt's schedule to meet the goal?

7

MAINTAINING COMMUNICATION

The steps outlined in the previous chapters are really just the beginning of your efforts to help parents and the community to understand performance-based assessment. In some ways what happens after you have carried out all of these recommendations is most important. How well you maintain communication with parents and your community will, after all, ultimately determine your success. This may be the ultimate challenge.

Providing information for families on skills required for students and implementing an interactive homework program are two of the practices recommended by Joyce Epstein (1995, p. 704) as part of a six-element schema for school and family connections. What she characterizes as "Type 4" involvement ("Learning at Home") also includes the following additional practices that can be part of your efforts to maintain communication about performance-based assessment:

- ♦ Calendars with activities for parents and students at home.

- ♦ Family math, science, and reading activities at school.

- ♦ Summer learning packets or activities.

The number of ways in which you can implement these ideas and others is only limited by your creativity and your ability to borrow the ideas of others! Creative educators have found some unique ways in which to get the message out about the exciting things that are happening in their schools. You should use all of them and seek others!

NEWSLETTERS

A newsletter is probably the easiest and most efficient way of maintaining continuous communication, and can serve as the mechanism whereby you get calendars with activities home to parents. Newsletters need not be long and detailed. In fact one sheet printed both front and back is probably a good length for a weekly newsletter. For monthly newsletters, two pages of paper printed on front and back of each, for a total of four pages, is probably adequate. Try to maintain the same masthead and some similar features in each newsletter, and remember to check the reading level of all material you send out. We also try to use the same color for each different publication to make it easier for parents to recognize important papers in children's book bags. When the communication is something *really* important, we use a brightly colored paper such as hot pink, sky blue, or pumpkin orange.

We established a newsletter for parents that specifically addresses performance-based assessment. It is called *Partners in Performance*. We tried to focus each issue on a different content area, and we included general information about the state tests and other important performance-based aspects of our instructional program. Articles in the first few issues included a list of things parents can do to help at home, explanations of acronyms we use to help students remember processes, sample writing prompts, sample visual organizers, lists of reading strategies, explanations of reading stances, and suggestions for strengthening thinking skills. Samples of the newsletter can be found in Figures 7.1 (p. 107) and 7.2 (p. 109) at the end of this chapter.

You may also want to explore the possibilities of contributing articles to the newsletters of other organizations in your community. Social services organizations, community service organizations, churches, and many other groups send newsletters to their constituents and may be a source of communication for you either regularly or occasionally.

Useful Contents for Newsletters

- **General information about tests**
- **Simple tasks using household materials**
- **Suggestions for using acronyms**
- **Graphic organizers**
- **Suggested writing topics**
- **Sample student responses**
- **Sample rubrics and other scoring tools**
- **Thinking skills challenge tasks (*Brain Teasers*)**

NEWSPAPER ARTICLES

The mass media is a source for widespread publicity of your efforts to improve the education of the children in your community. Most publishers are interested in anything that is different from the ordinary, and will be willing to publish concise, information-rich articles on educational topics. It is probably wise to keep articles on performance-based assessment short and to the point, with careful attention to fact and not opinion. Expect to receive some sharp criticism in the editorial section following the publication of your first article, and be very careful not to respond defensively. It has been our experience that adults who do not themselves have children in school, sometimes tend to be the most critical of educational change. An article in the local newspaper may be their first association with the new ideas. Figure 7.3 (pp. 98–102) is a series of possible newspaper articles on performance-based assessment.

(Text continues on page 103.)

FIGURE 7.3 SAMPLE NEWSPAPER ARTICLES

ARTICLE 1: WHAT IS PERFORMANCE-BASED ASSESSMENT?

What do adults think of when they hear the word "test"? For over 60 years, American schools have relied almost exclusively on multiple-choice tests to determine if and how much students have learned. There are many reasons why we have had this dependence. Multiple-choice tests are perceived to be objective. There is only one correct answer and students either select that answer or they don't. Multiple-choice tests are easy to administer and easy to score, especially if the teacher has access to an electronic scanner and computer programs for this purpose. Multiple-choice tests are also relatively easy to develop.

In recent years it has become evident that our reliance on multiple-choice tests has led to numerous problems. Some of these problems stem from the nature of the tests themselves, and some arise from changes in our expectations for student success.

We now realize that multiple-choice tests are not as objective as we thought. If fact, they are fundamentally *subjective* in the sense that someone has to decide what is tested, and in that occasionally there can be a difference of opinion regarding the correct answer. There is no room for individual interpretation of test items and no allowance for levels of student learning in multiple-choice tests. All students must understand and interpret the questions equally well, and all students must be able to respond with the same level of mastery. There is no allowance for individual differences in learning rate or learning style. There is little feedback available to either teachers or students when the student does not show full mastery.

In addition, the content of school curriculums has broadened to include skills that cannot be assessed appropriately with multiple-choice test items. Learning science, for instance, no longer involves simply a body of facts and principles that must be memorized and recalled. Science now involves learning how to set up and conduct an experiment, learning how to use the tools of science, learning how to observe and record scientific phenomena, and many other active, demonstrable skills.

In order to appropriately determine if students have mastered the skills they have been taught, an assessment must be used which requires them to *demonstrate* their level of mastery. True, there are elements of knowledge and understanding that underlie these skills which can be appropriately assessed with multiple-choice tests.

However, effective (valid and reliable) assessment of the skills themselves requires a different approach.

Performance-based assessment provides this type of evaluation. When the assessment requires students to demonstrate in a realistic and appropriate context the level at which they have mastered the skills that have been taught, assessment is more meaningful and more indicative of learning. There is room for individual differences in learning rate and learning style and there is rich feedback, making performance-based assessment a valuable tool for education in the 21st century.

ARTICLE 2: WHAT ARE THE CHARACTERISTICS OF PERFORMANCE-BASED ASSESSMENT?

If you ask a group of adults if they have ever participated in a performance-based assessment, most of them will probably say that they have not. It is a common mistake to assume that this method of assessment is something new. In fact, anyone who has a driver's license has been assessed using performance-based assessment, which comprises the vast majority of the U.S. adult population.

Performance-based assessment involves a respondent performing a specified activity or creating a product while an evaluator observes and then judges the level of achievement. This type of assessment has long been in use in many disciplines in schools, such as the arts, physical education, speech, and theatre. It is also an important part of the certification process in many occupations. Nobody wants to fly in an airplane piloted by someone who has demonstrated their ability to fly the plane by simply answering some multiple-choice questions! Moreover, the performance-based assessment must have been conducted in an authentic context—one that simulates the real world with all of its challenges.

Performance-based assessments used in schools are similar in many ways to assessments used in the world of work. Students are asked to demonstrate mastery of the skills and processes taught by performing the skills on demand. Performance is judged against a set of standards determined in advance by the teacher. If the performance does not meet the standards for accomplishment that are considered to be indicative of mastery, the teacher is able to tell what needs to be improved by looking at the standards and comparing the current performance to the expectations. Then the student receives specific, useful feedback about the performance.

In schools, students are usually asked to demonstrate mastery of skills within a context that is called *authentic*. This means that the teacher sets up a hypothetical situation that could actually occur in the *real* world and asks the students to apply the skills they have learned to a realistic problem. An example would be pretending that the class is going to have an ice cream party and asking the students to determine how much ice cream will be needed, conduct a survey to determine the most popular flavor, graph the results of the survey, and calculate how much the ice cream will cost.

Teachers generally use scoring tools called *rubrics* to evaluate students' achievement on performance-based tasks. A rubric outlines levels of expectation for quality performance. The expectations are published in advance so that students can use them as guidelines while completing the task. The teacher then judges the quality of the performance against the expectations and assigns a grade.

If a student's grade is not what was expected, the student and teacher can look at the rubric together and decide what the student needs to do to assure improvement of performance. In this way, students have a great deal of control over their own grades and are motivated to work harder to do their personal best.

ARTICLE 3: HOW DOES PERFORMANCE-BASED ASSESSMENT IMPACT THE EDUCATIONAL PROGRAM?

Many parents have noticed that the nature of homework has changed. Questions that follow a reading assignment require critical thinking rather than simple recall of facts. Math problems are followed by the requirement to justify the answer or explain how the answer was achieved. Spelling words are used in sentences instead of simply being memorized.

What has caused these and other changes? Why are they necessary? And what can parents do to help their children meet the challenges of new expectations?

Performance-based learning has always been an important part of formative education. Knowing how to do a pushup without injuring oneself was never enough. We had to show the physical education teacher we knew how *and could do it.* Knowing how a button is supposed to be sewn on was also never enough. We had to show the home arts teacher that we knew how *and could do it.*

Over the years educators have realized that there are many skills in the content areas of reading, mathematics, science and social studies that similarly need to be *demonstrated.* Knowing how something is supposed to be done and being able to recognize the component parts or the steps in the process on a multiple-choice test is not good enough. In order for everyone involved in the learning process to be sure students *can do* what they have learned *to do*, teachers have to demonstrate the skills, students have to practice them, and students have *to do* them during assessments.

For instance, if we want students to be able to think critically, we have to demonstrate critical thinking, give them plenty of opportunities to practice it, and expect them to do it on assessments.

If we want students to be able to independently solve problems, we have to show them the steps in the problem-solving process, teach them how to analyze each step in the process, and ask them to carry out the process on assessments. It is not enough to let them recognize the steps in the process or choose the correct answer to the problem out of a list of four or five possibilities. Life is not a multiple-choice test. It does not present us with lists of possible solutions to our problems.

School curriculums and teaching strategies have been adapting in recent years to enable our changing expectations for what students should know and be able to do. Content is more frequently presented in realistic contexts so that students are able to understand the meaning and usefulness of what they are learning. Students and teachers alike are expected to think *outside of the box* by going beyond defining, describing, identifying, labeling, locating, reciting, naming, and stating information. More often they are expected to explain, interpret, apply, adapt, analyze, construct, hypothesize, judge, evaluate, appraise, justify, and support.

All of these changes are helping students prepare themselves better for the twenty-first century. They are learning to learn rather than simply absorbing information.

ARTICLE 4: WHAT CAN BE DONE TO HELP STUDENTS SUCCEED ON PERFORMANCE-BASED ASSESSMENTS?

Parents are their children's first teachers. How do they know what to do when they are teaching their children? Basically, they rely on what they experienced themselves as children, and they do what comes naturally.

Sometimes parents become frustrated, however, when a battle ensues over the kitchen table because the parent thinks something should be done one way and the child is certain that, "My teacher said to do it *this* way." Unfortunately, the focus on performance-based learning in our schools is causing this situation to occur more often.

Studying for tests can be especially problematic. When multiple-choice tests were the norm, studying was largely a matter of repeating information over and over until it was memorized. The parent's job was to provide support for the drilling and practicing that was required to ensure that the information could be recalled during the test.

Students studying for performance-based assessments must go well beyond the drilling and practice. They must be able to *demonstrate* mastery of the concepts, often by carrying out a process within a limited amount of time, creating a product according to specific criteria, or justifying the solutions they find. Studying becomes an active process when these are the expectations.

Parents can help their children adapt to the changing expectations of today's assessments by doing some of the following things.

1. Encourage critical reading. Talk to your child about what your child has read and ask questions that require your child to go beyond recalling information that can be found directly in the text.

2. Provide tools for mathematics work. A ruler, compass, calculator, number cubes, graph paper, and a protractor may be appropriate depending on what grade your child is in. Ask you child's teacher for ideas.

3. Help your child learn to be observant, especially in the area of science. Discuss things your child observes and help him or her describe the properties, characteristics, and results of things that happen.

4. Help your child learn to summarize in writing things he or she has read, done, or observed. Students also need practice putting ideas and definitions into their own words.

5. Remind your child to use charts and diagrams to help organize his or her thoughts. There are many types of *visual organizers* used in schools today. Ask your child's teacher for suggestions about which ones are most often used in your child's classroom.

6. Encourage your child to relate things that are currently being learned to prior knowledge. Thinking about what he or she already knows about a topic or problem is an important first step in any problem-solving situation.

OTHER SOURCES OF
WIDESPREAD AUDIENCES

The wider you throw your net, the greater will be your network of support. Don't forget the community in general, and the other professionals in your community who have a vested interest in the education of the community's youth. Professional offices of doctors, dentists, and veterinarians, sport and fitness facilities, restaurants, social services agencies, and other places where families go and have the opportunity to pick up and read printed information are excellent places to start your partnership efforts.

Although we have not tried this strategy, some school districts have made agreements with local fast-food restaurants to use tray liners provided by the school system on which there is a brief description of the new assessment program. If this strategy is attempted, there should definitely be a note on the document telling where those who wish additional information can get it.

PARENT VOLUNTEER PROGRAMS

The value of parent volunteer programs cannot be overemphasized. When parents are actually in the classroom, observing what goes on and how concepts are taught, there is continuous and meaningful benefit for all concerned. Teachers serve as models for the innovative methodology and parents learn by seeing strategies put into practice in consistent, straightforward ways. Some schools have used volunteering as a means to build their support base by making a concerted effort to place doubtful parents in the classrooms of teachers who are using the new methodology with great success.

You might also focus your training efforts on your volunteers before extending them to the general parent population. This would increase your cadre of parents who are either *expert* or *competent* instructors and would give you a firm base of support among parents in general.

COVERING ALL THE BASES

Lastly, a few words are needed about some situations that may require unique approaches as you work toward making connections with parents and your community. There are a number of groups of parents and community members that require differential approaches for one reason or another and not all schools have the same types of groups.

It is important to recognize how different families are in the twenty-first century. Most students do not live in a *traditional* family these days. Epstein and Scott-Jones (1993, pp. 17–29) have outlined numerous family members for whom there are special implications when planning home and school connections. These groups include:

- Parents who are younger than average
- Parents who are older than average
- Families of students in upper grades
- Less-educated parents
- Limited-English-Proficient families
- Single parents
- Stepparents and blended families
- Non-custodial parents
- Foster parents
- Families of adolescent parents
- Parents who work outside the home
- Families of students new to the school
- Families of students bussed to school

As you implement your plans for helping parents and the community to understand performance-based assessment, it is important to make sure you have considered your school population and made special efforts to adapt your presentations and materials appropriately if you have a considerable number of individuals in any of these groups. This may be more true for some groups than others. Since there are a few groups for whom the suggestions in this book may need to be adapted, a few suggestions might be helpful.

PARENTS WHO ARE YOUNGER THAN AVERAGE

Parents who are younger than average may believe that the schools failed them. They may fear that the schools will fail their children as well. They may be even further discouraged once they find out that things are very different from what they remember about school, especially in the area of assessment.

Younger parents are often reluctant to come to school. They may need an individual invitation to participate in activities. They also may have less self-confidence than other parents and, even though they went through school themselves more recently than some other parents, they may need more assistance learning new skills than other parents will. This group of parents may not respond as well to having their children with them when they participate in your first family activity, so you may want to be ready to provide more guidance for them as they work through the activities.

PARENTS WHO ARE
OLDER THAN AVERAGE

Parents who are older than average may be more involved in careers and activities outside of the home. They may have little time available to become involved in school activities, and may need alternative means to learn the new skills. For these parents, the interactive homework assignments you use during the last step in the process may be the most instructive of all your efforts. For that reason, follow-up by phone or during parent/teacher conferences may be very useful.

It is also possible that the child of older parents attending your school is the youngest of many children, which means the parents have a long history of involvement with all aspects of education. Since their information may be outdated, they may actually be more in need of information about new strategies than the average parent. This presents a special challenge if they cannot attend meetings and workshops, because they may be the most likely to use strategies at home that are actually counterproductive to the newer strategies.

FAMILIES OF STUDENTS
IN UPPER GRADES

There is some evidence that parents' feelings of inadequacy to help may increase as their children get older (Epstein, 1991, p. 271). In some cases the literacy skills of the children may have surpassed the skills of their parents. You may therefore need to give more help to parents of children in the upper grades than to parents of children in the lower grades. These parents may also need to be reassured that their help is useful and valued.

FAMILIES WITH LIMITED
ENGLISH PROFICIENCY

If you have a significant population of Limited-English-Proficient families and you want them to participate, you will need to provide translators at your meetings, and print your handbook, handouts, and interactive homework activities in appropriate languages other than English.

PARENTS WHO WORK
OUTSIDE THE HOME

Those of us who work in schools and have better than average access to our own children's school activities tend to forget that the rest of the working world may not be as fortunate as we are. Many employers will not allow employees to take off any less than a full day of work, and leave, other than sick leave, can work against them in terms of promotions and transfers. There are also many parents who work shifts and just cannot get away from their jobs to attend activities in school.

You might want to explore options such as videotaping presentations so that tapes can be sent home to families who show interest in attending activities but cannot get time off to do so. If you make videotapes, make sure you build in the pauses needed to allow parents and students to work on the tasks at appropriate points in the presentation.

You could also establish a school web page and put customized (even interactive) workshops on the Internet that parents could access at any time of the day or night. A chat room or question-and-answer service would also be a good idea. These kinds of strategies make information accessible to a greater number of people and let your school community know that you are anxious to share ideas and strategies with everyone, even those who work at all hours.

New Families

Special attention should be paid to new families. They need to be caught up on the new initiatives and given the same opportunities that have been provided to parents during the course of the school year. It may be helpful to save copies of all parent communications and make them available to new parents when they register their children. You do not necessarily need to provide *all* materials to every new parent, but having things available for examination and being willing to provide copies of materials will be seen as a benefit to those arriving in the middle of things.

FIGURE 7.1 SAMPLE NEWSLETTER NO. 1

Partners in Performance

A Newsletter about Performance Assessment for Use at Home

| Volume 1, No. 1 | Calvert County Public Schools | December 1997 |

WELCOME to *Partners in Performance* and its premiere issue. We recognize the essential role that the home plays in a child's success, so we want you to know more about what your youngster is doing in the hours at school. That way, we can all talk the same talk!

While the info in *Partners in Performance* should be useful for students in any grade, only certain grades will receive copies to go home because of the cost involved. So, the assessed grades for MSPAP *and* the grades just prior to those—where there's the most intensive preparation—are targeted. If you have a child in grades 2-5 or in grades 7 or 8, you can expect four issues of *Partners in Performance* to arrive home in your child's backpack this year.

Each issue will feature a different skill or content area. You'll get some info on the "what" and the "why," along with some related strategies that you can do at home. Maybe *Partners in Performance* will decorate a few refrigerators, becoming something you can use throughout the year.

WHAT CAN YOU DO TO HELP AT HOME?

- Recognize that writing is a tool for learning, not just a demonstration of what has been learned.
- Make ideas "stationary" by putting them on paper. It encourages thinking.
- Foster writing at home—listmaking, oral history, or letter writing. Take dictation and transcribe it.
- Encourage note-taking while on trips—even to the store. Notice details!
- Ignore mistakes if possible; highlight the positive. Focus on *what* was said rather than *how* it was written.
- Be specific with praise—details, title, expression, accuracy, description, insight, imagination, whatever—and articulate reasons for your approval. Give your youngster valid reasons to be confident about himself as a writer.
- "Publish" on the refrigerator or in e-mail correspondence.
- Discuss your own writing—whether it's a note to the teacher or a memo from work. Better yet, let your youngster see you struggle with words and how you conquer them.
- Play with words—games, puzzles, tongue-twisters, rhymes, word poems, free associations. Have fun and encourage thinking!

You have a unique role in your youngster's life. You can give individualized attention, not only helping, but also listening and

---

Writing is simply putting thoughts into a permanent form—with words, illustrations, graphs, etc. Being able to communicate without actually being present is an important skill—not only in school but in life. No matter what our roles in life, we write—lists, letters, reports.

Probably, most tests you took in school asked you to choose a letter or to write a short answer. Today's tests—whether classroom, MSPAP, or the proposed high school end-of-course exams—require students to do a lot of writing. And it's not just "stating the answer" that tests are expecting. Students often have to explain the "how" or "why" of something or to justify or support their answers. Writing is a very important skill for youngsters to have.

Good writing looks different in different situations. Knowing the purpose and the audience of readers helps focus the writing. A panoramic view of the location won't work when a close-up shot of a detail is needed. When writing is more than just a listing of ideas or a brief response, the best results happen when the writing process takes place.

- The preliminary step in the writing process is knowing exactly what to do. This is so basic that sometimes it's overlooked. What a mistake! If you don't know exactly what the end result is supposed to be, it's easy to miss the target.

FAT PIG is a helpful "trick" that has moved Calvert County into the top ranks of Maryland test-takers. This acronym "unlocks" an assignment so students can identify what they need to have:

*F*orm (paragraph, essay, graph, illustration, etc.)

*A*udience (intended reader or viewer of the finished product)

*T*opic (the main idea or point or focus)

*P*urpose (explain, inform, persuade, entertain, etc.)

*I*nformation *G*uide (subtopics or elements to be included or developed)

Identifying the Information Guide is crucial; the topic alone isn't enough. If you're asked to bring food to a party, it makes a big difference if someone's expecting appetizers or dessert. Here's

what it looks like when students use the FAT PIG to unlock an assignment:

SAMPLE PROMPT: Suppose your class has been discussing *problems that some youngsters in Calvert County encounter*. You decide to write a *business letter* to the editor of the local newspaper, *informing* the *readers of the newspaper what the problem is* and *what you think causes it*. Inform them of *how youngsters are affected* and *suggest some solutions to the problem*.

---

*F*orm = business letter

*A*udience = readers of the newspaper

*T*opic = problems that some youngsters in Calvert County encounter

*P*urpose = informing

*I*nformation *G*uide = ① what the problem is ② what you think causes it ③ how youngsters are affected and ④ some solutions to the problem

- The first real step of the writing process is pre-writing. Good writing starts with the head, not with the hand.

The goal is to consider ideas and then select what to include and how to arrange it. It's sort of like looking at what's available, whether in a store or a buffet line. Consider options and then make choices.

Brainstorm ideas—no criticism allowed! List as many ideas as possible and then think like a film director. Which idea works best for developing the picture the reader should "see"? Actually drawing their ideas helps some youngsters. They literally focus the picture for themselves.

Once writers have made a choice, they can begin the planning stage of pre-writing: choosing what to include and how to arrange it. The planning stage is difficult for many kids—they want to "just get into it and see what happens." Sometimes they need to do that kind of "free write" or "garbage write" for getting their ideas out and then looking through them for anything worth saving, but that's part of considering ideas, not actually planning the product.

"Four Squares" is a sure-fire way to organize and develop the plan:

✔ Fold a sheet of loose leaf paper into fourths.
✔ State your topic or thesis in the margin at the top.

✔ Organize each part of the Information Guide by writing it at the top of a box.
✔ Number the lines in each box for as many points or details as you expect should be developed (3 or 5, perhaps). Use only one or two words to list each point.

Lack of Indoor Soccer Facilities	
Problem	Causes for problem
1. many potential players 2. few places 3. active game 4. large teams 5.	1. no public facilities 2. presumed damage 3. poor PR 4. 5.
How people are affected	Possible solutions
1. travel far 2. long time 3. miss homework 4. family hardships 5. large teams 6. little practice	1. determine actual damage 2. insurance for damage 3. preventative measures 4. higher fees 5. skating rink 6. new companies

- Next comes the drafting stage. Like working with clay, the goal is to shape the product into something recognizable. It's not supposed to be finished yet—lots of reshaping will take place. And like clay, the rough draft of the writing will probably be messy. That's OK—there's an artist at work!

If your youngster has a problem developing ideas, suggest using separate sides of paper—one side for each part of the Information Guide. That encourages organization and elaboration. (Fold the Four Squares paper so that the writer looks only at one box when writing that part of the rough draft.) The topic and the subtopic of the Information Guide are ready to develop into main idea and topic sentences. Each point or detail in a box expands into a complete sentence or example.

- The next stage in the writing process is re vision. That's right—"revision" has been broken apart to emphasize taking a second view of what's actually on the paper to see what works and what doesn't. Make no mistake—it's not editing. Don't waste time on "fixing" the errors in "the buoy whent to the stur" The problems aren't punctuation and spelling. The real problem is that the sentence doesn't develop a picture for the reader. Identifying where and how to create images is what revision is all about. Eventually editing the mistakes in "Matt pedaled his bycicle to the farmacy for his grandpa's heart medicine" is worth doing!

The trick to revision is to make sure the writing stayed on Topic, has Organization so the reader has an easy "ride," and provides enough Development of the images the author had in mind. The DOT structures an objective view for the writer:

➤ Underline where you've stated the <u>Topic</u> (topic sentence, thesis, maybe just the title).

➤ Box in ⌐each⌐ ⌐part⌐ of the Information Guide.

➤ Count each aspect of Development, such as the number of sentences or details.

Once writers discover what's actually on their paper, it's easier for them to determine where and why to revise. Changes go right on the draft itself. Including arrows or numbers keeps the ideas straight. Don't expect a revised rough draft to look anything but rough. If the paper looks like a fat pig actually crossed it, then probably enough changes are in place.

- Editing—the final stage—often meets with resistance. When youngsters finish the page, they often think they've finished the work. Not only are they generally too close to their effort; they're also too possessive of it. How can you help novice writers distance themselves as readers?

If at all possible, literally provide a little distance—in time. Wait until after another activity or even until the next day to encourage *active proofreading*. Writers read their papers aloud. The key here is not reading for a partner's benefit but simply to focus on individual words by slowing down enough to read each and every word aloud. Reading silently won't work; reading aloud does. Fix mistakes on the final copy itself. It's rare that a finished piece of writing needs to be "pretty"; it ought to be correct.

FIGURE 7.2 SAMPLE NEWSLETTER NO. 2

Partners in Performance

A Newsletter about Performance Assessment for the Home

Volume 1, No. 2   Calvert County Public Schools   April 1998

One of the most magical journeys anyone can undertake is learning to read. When we learn how to make sense of what's on a page—whether it's words, a graph, an illustration, or a musical score—we've unlocked the potential of an entire universe.

You may have heard that reading scores in many schools throughout Maryland, as measured by MSPAP, are lower than people expected. Like almost everyone else, you're probably wondering what that means, especially since your youngster is probably a pretty good reader. What's the problem? And what are Calvert County schools doing about it?

First, let's recognize what MSPAP reading entails. In MSPAP, the *constructing meaning* that most of us consider "reading" is just the beginning phase. MSPAP expects readers to go beyond what is literally on the page. They read "between the lines" to make inferences or predictions or to draw conclusions—readers *extend meaning* beyond the literal words.

MSPAP also demands that students extend their ability to interpret (whether a poem, a photograph, a chart, a news article, or a set of directions) to make comparisons and connections to their own ideas or experiences. Even that's not enough; students *examine meaning*—scrutinizing the author's organization of ideas, choice of words, even the inclusion of visual information. What a difference from just figuring out what the words man!

Can you help youngsters make the leap from decoders to sophisticated perusers of print? Absolutely! For beginning readers, you already know it's essential for kids to read and to receive praise for reading. What about older, more proficient readers? Learning how to develop a solid interpretation with explicit evidence from the text requires increasing sophistication. You can help throughout your youngster's entire school career.

Good readers *interact* with the text, often unaware that they're doing so. Model this interaction at home. (OK, you'll probably feel self-conscious at first.) Simply say out loud those barely conscious thoughts that occur when you're reading something important to you. As you find a place in the text that surprises you, say so. Voice your confusion when something doesn't make sense. Explicitly identify important points. Make connections with what you already know or what you learn as you read. Show that reading *involves* you; it's more than just knowing the words on a page.

There's more you can do to help. When you're aware of what occurs in classroom instruction, the more opportunities you can find for one-on-one reinforcement.

Because reading is a process, there are specific strategies to use before, during, and after reading. Using these strategies aids comprehension.

One CCPS teacher created the **LAMP** to "turn on the light" for his students *before* they do their actual reading:

◆ **L**ook at the title, illustrations, or captions.

◆ **A**ccess prior knowledge: What do I already know?

◆ **M**ake predictions: What do I expect to find out?

◆ **P**urpose: What purpose am I reading for?

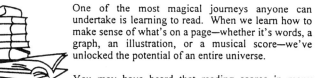

Following those initial steps sets the stage for proficient reading.

"During reading" strategies are important too. You're using "during" strategies if you do any of the following:

➤ When reading directions do you go back to the text to be sure you have the right amount or the correct part?

➤ Do you visualize any of the steps you need to follow?

➤ Perhaps you find yourself confused by something on the page—Do you go back to a previous part to clear up the confusion?

➤ Do you adjust your reading speed according to your purpose or the text difficulty?

While you may take all these interactions with the text for granted, your child may not recognize that good reading is more than proceeding steadfastly from word to word. Consciously noting when you understand and when you don't understand is a crucial skill to develop.

Here are other strategies while reading the text itself:

➤ Paraphrase what the author said.

➤ Predict what you expect the article to state next.

➤ Make connections between the novel—or even a set of instructions—and your own experience.

➤ Compare, draw conclusions and make inferences.

Do you do any of these things? If so, you're doing a good job of monitoring your understanding, verifying and clarifying what you've read. Let your youngster in on these tactics, too!

And yes, there are strategies to use after reading:

➤ Can you summarize what you read?
➤ Did it make sense?
➤ Did you accomplish your purpose for reading?
  ◇ Does the bookshelf you assembled look like the illustration on the box?
  ◇ Did the travel brochure answer all your questions about a vacation there?
  ◇ Maybe you wanted to escape into a good novel—Did you hate returning to reality?

After reading, you may not even think about reflection, but it's important too. What specific strategies did you use as you read? Before saying, "I didn't use any," think back to the "during" list; you probably reread some part or perhaps changed your speed. Let your youngster know that those strategies aren't just "school stuff."

Using strategies during the reading process is only part of the answer for improving reading. One specific approach we're using in Calvert County for improving MSPAP scores is recognizing the importance of the "stance" questions.

Although there are many possible purposes for reading, MSPAP assesses only three—Reading to Be Informed, Reading to Perform a Task, and Reading for Literary Experience—all very useful purposes for life-long readers.

MSPAP uses four stances or vantage points for gaining insight into the text. These stances are the same for each of the three purposes.

Global Understanding focuses the "big picture" to get an overall impression:

✔ What's the selection about?

✔ What was the author's purpose?

Developing Interpretation zooms in on the "bits and pieces" of the text to verify and clarify the reader's perceptions:

✔ Paraphrase a part of the text or retell what the text says.

✔ Based on the text, make an inference or a prediction or draw a conclusion

Personal Reflection asks readers to connect their own lives and experiences and the text itself:

✔ Compare a character, an event or an idea from the text to your own life or experience.

✔ Identify new information you have learned or additional information you would like.

Think of *Critical Stance* as "Author's Craft." The focus changes from the "picture" to the "picture-maker," asking the reader to examine and speculate how or why the author did something:

✔ How did the author keep our interest?

✔ What did the author need to know to write this?

✔ Rewrite the text for a different audience.

You may find that your youngster is becoming increasingly comfortable with analyzing the literary quality of any text—not just a short story (reading for literary experience), but also a news article (reading to be informed) or science lab procedures (reading to perform a task)—through these four stances. Most adults aren't used to speculating about "how" or "why" an author created an effect, yet MSPAP expects readers as young as third graders to do so. Before you snort, "That's ridiculous!" think about the implications here for improving thinking skills! The problem with the state's MSPAP reading scores is not our kids' reading abilities; they must have experience with the kinds of questions they will need to answer.

Discussing ideas with your youngsters can be a huge help. And although we most often think of reading as being about words on a page, developing the ability to interpret is much more than that. All these strategies and stances apply equally as well to visual communication, whether it's a TV show or a cartoon strip. The possibilities are limitless. You have a unique role in your youngster's life—enjoy!

REFERENCES

Barclay, K., & Boone, E. (1996). *The parent difference: Uniting school, family, and community.* Arlington Heights, IL: IRI SkyLight.

Covey, S. R. (1989). *The 7 habits of highly effective people.* New York: Simon and Schuster.

Delgado-Gaitan, C. (1990). *Literacy for empowerment: The role of parents in children's education.* New York: The Falmer Press.

Epstein, J. (1986). Parents' reactions to teacher practices of parent involvement. *The Elementary School Journal, 86* (3), 277–294.

Epstein, J. (1990). Parent involvement: Theory, research, and implications for integrating sociologies of education and family. In D. G. Unger & M. B. Sussman (Eds.), *Families in community settings: Interdisciplinary perspectives.* New York: Haworth Press.

Epstein, J. (1991). Effects on student achievement of teachers' practices of parent involvement. *Advances in Reading/Language Research, 5,* 261–276.

Epstein, J. (1992). *Summary: Teachers involve parents in schoolwork (TIPS): Involving families to improve student achievement.* Baltimore: Center on Families, Communities, Schools and Children's Learning, The Johns Hopkins University.

Epstein, J. (1993). School and family partnerships. Introducing a new instructor series. *Instructor, 103*(2), 73–76.

Epstein, J. (1995). School/family/community partnerships: Caring for the children we share. *Phi Delta Kappan, 76*(9), 701–712.

Epstein, J., & Scott-Jones, D. (1993). Schools, family, and community connections for accelerating student progress in elementary and middle grades. In H. M. Levin (Ed.), *Accelerating the education of at-risk students.* Philadelphia: Falmer.

Epstein, J. K., Simon, B., & Salinas K. C. (1997). Involving parents in homework in the middle grades. *Phi Delta Kappa Research Bulletin No. 18.* Bloomington, IN: Center for Evaluation, Development, and Research, Phi Delta Kappa International.

Fruchter, N., Galletta, A., & White, J. L. (1993). New directions in parent involvement. *Equity and Choice, 9 (3),* 33–43.

Henderson, A. T., Marburger, C. T., & Ooms, T. (1987). *The evidence continues to grow: Parent involvement improves student achievement.* Columbia, MD: National Committee for Citizens in Education.

Jones, L. T. (1991). *Strategies for involving parents in their children's education: Fastback 315.* Bloomington, IN: Phi Delta Kappa Educational Foundation.

Kahn, M. B. (1996). Parental involvement in education: Possibilities and limitations. *The School Community Journal, 6* (1), 57–68.

McGilp, J., & Michael, M. (1994). *The home-school connection: Guidelines for working with parents.* Portsmouth, NH: Heinemann.

Rich, D., & Jones, C. (1985). *The forgotten factor in school success: The family: A policy-maker's guide.* Washington, DC: The Home and School Institute.

Rioux, J. W., & Berla, N. (1993). *Innovations in parent & family involvement.* Larchmont, NY: Eye on Education.

BIBLIOGRAPHY

Alvy, K. T. (1994). *Parent training today: A social necessity.* Studio City, CA: Center for the Improvement of Child Caring.

Batey, C. S. (1996). *Parents are lifesavers: A handbook for parent involvement in schools.* Thousand Oaks, CA: Corwin Press.

Burns, R. C. (Ed.). (1993). *Parents and schools: From visitors to partners.* Washington, D. C.: National Education Association.

Edwards, P. A., &. Young, L. S. (1992). Beyond parents: Family, community, and school involvement. *Phi Delta Kappan, 74* (1), 72–80.

Epstein, J., Salinas, C., & Jackson, V. E. (1992). *TIPS: Interactive homework in language arts prototype activities, grade6.* Baltimore, MD: Center on Families, Communities, Schools and Children's Learning, The Johns Hopkins University.

Fuller, M. L., & Olsen, G. (1998). *Home-school relations.* Boston: Allyn and Bacon.

Gareau, M., & Sawatzky, D. (1995). Parents and schools working together: A qualitative study of parent-school collaboration. *The Alberta Journal of Educational Research, 61* (4), 462-473.

Gestwicki, C. (1992). *Home, school and community relations: A guide to working with parents* (2nd Ed.). Albany, NY: Delmar Publishers.

Gutloff, K. (1997). Make it happen: Five strategies for reaching the hard-to-reach parent. *NEA Today, 16* (3), 4–5.

Henderson, A. T., Marburger, C. T., & Ooms, T. (1989). *Beyond the bake sale: An educator's guide to working with parents.* Columbia, MD: National Committee for Citizens in Education.

Hoover-Dempsey, K. V., & Sandler, H. M. (1995). Parental involvement in children's education: Why does it make a difference? *Teachers College Record, 97* (2), 310–331.

Knight, B. J. (1987). *Parent involvement assumptions.* Position paper. Manhattan Beach, CA: Manhattan Beach Intermediate School.

Loucks, H. (1992). Increasing parent/family involvement: Ten ideas that work. *NASSP Bulletin, 76* (543), 19–23.

Lyons, P., Robbins, A., & Smith, A. (1983). *Involving parents: A handbook for participation in schools.* Ypsilanti, MI: The High Scope Press.

MacPherson, A. (1993). Parent-professional partnership: A review and discussion of issues. *Early Child Development and Care, 86,* 61–77.

Mannan, G., & Blackwell, J. (1992). Parent involvement: Barriers and opportunities. *The Urban Review, 24* (3), 219–226.

Meadows, B. J. (1993). Through the eyes of parents. *Educational Leadership, 51* (2), 31–34.

National Coalition for Parent Involvement in Education. (1994). *Developing family/school partnerships: Guidelines for schools and school districts.* Washington, DC: National Education Association.

National Education Association. (1996). *Building Parent Partnerships.* Washington, DC: National Education Association.

National Parents' Day Coalition. (1998). *The ABC's of parent involvement in education.* Washington, DC: author.

Partnership for Family Involvement in Education. (1998). *Overview of research on family involvement in children's learning.* www.ed.gov/PFIE/Conrsrch.html.

Rich, D., & Jones, C. (1977). *Education: A family matter.* Washington, DC: Home and School Institute and Trinity College.

Shockley, B., Michalove, B., & Allen, J. (1995). *Engaging families: Connecting home and school literacy communities.* Portsmouth, NH: Heinemann.

St. John, E. P. (1995). Parents and school reform. *Journal for a Just and Caring Education, 1* (1), 80–97.